Starting in the Middle

Starting
in the Middle

Judith Wax

Holt, Rinehart and Winston · New York

Published by Holt, Rinehart and Winston, 383 Madison
Avenue, New York, New York 10017.
Published simultaneously in Canada by Holt, Rinehart
and Winston of Canada, Limited.

Library of Congress Cataloging in Publication Data

Wax, Judith.
Starting in the middle.

1. Wax, Judith.   2. Middle aged women—United
States—Biography.   I. Title.
HQ1413.W38A37   301.43'4   78-16809

ISBN: 0-03-020296-5

DESIGNER: Joy Chu

Printed in the United States of America
10 9 8 7 6 5 4

Grateful acknowledgment is made for use of the
following:

One line from "Into the Stone" from *Poems 1957–1967*
by James Dickey, copyright © 1960 by James Dickey.
Reprinted by permission of Wesleyan University Press.

For Shel

*For their encouragement, special thanks to
Robie Macauley, Judy Gingold, Pat Berens,
Wendy Moonan, Paul and Claudia Wax,
and—most of all—Jennifer Josephy, my editor.*

Contents

Starting in the Middle

Introduction

A funny thing happened to me on the way to menopause. Lots of funny things did—not only to me, but to people I know, fellow travelers on that involuntary pilgrimage into middle age. Which doesn't mean it's all been galloping euphoria. As one friend who's been making the journey with more than her share of motion sickness says, "Sometimes life is so rotten, I don't know why they don't just let you phone it in."

Remember Lorenzo Jones and his wife, Belle? Back in the forties, when my idea of ecstasy was parlaying a few sneezes into a schoolday spent in bed listening to radio soaps, I learned all I thought I'd ever need to know about midlife turbulence from the Lorenzo Jones announcer. Even now in my head I often hear that mellifluous voice intoning, "But somehow with Lorenzo, there are more smiles . . . than tears." I'm not sure how many of my friends today could keep up with the Joneses' happiness-to-grief ratio, but then, the road to middle age (perhaps you've noticed) is a lot more perilous since Lorenzo and Belle bumbled by on it.

For those purists who demand sounder philosophical departure points than forties soap opera, Kierkegaard's always good, at lending weight to a slender premise. Taking his name in vain can get you parodied in a Woody Allen movie, so I'll only do it once with his "Life must be understood backward." But at a time in life when many of us are sandwiched between feelings of responsibility toward not-quite-autonomous children and aging parents (and maybe blinkered by our own seventies meism), upheavals on the present landscape can obscure the backward glance. At forty-seven, I have trouble enough with the first glimpse in the mirror some mornings, never mind panoramic appraisals.

"For God's sake," says my mother-the-Hungarian, "why do you always have to reveal your age?" And each time I mention those offending digits in an article I write, I hear from my mother-in-law, too—another long-distance protester. "When they run your picture," she counsels, "you don't always *look* that old."

Though it's almost a point of honor with me to unbutton my birthdays publicly, I mind the way they're adding up. And I mind even more that I *do* mind. Maybe, given my Budapest heritage, age anxiety comes with the genes, but you don't need blood of the Gabors to suffer from it. After all, we live in a country where one can hear, as I did recently, a TV host ask a white-haired game contestant, "What did you do in your lifetime?" No one seemed to notice the implication, not even when he said it again (it was "Senior Day") to the next older-than-springtime guest. The distressing part was that the host's gaffe probably went unnoticed because he'd blurted out what most of us think automatically: that to be past certified

2

prime is to be past life itself. So if, in our forties and fifties, intimations of obsolescence goose—at least occasionally—even those among us with altered consciousnesses and Vienna-tailored psyches, it could hardly be otherwise. When I counted the number of toupees at an East Coast gathering of psychiatrists who were discussing how to help people cope with getting older, I suspected that doctrine and dismay are only a hairsbreadth apart (and vanity androgynous).

"Look! We Have Come Through!" D. H. Lawrence once exulted in a series of poems. I couldn't put such a confident title on my own rites of passage, but to have ricocheted through the last few decades of American life and come to middle age ready for more (nothing fancy, though, and rights of refusal would be nice) confers moments of sneaky exhilaration. To say that we have been an assaulted generation is fair, I think, if self-justifying. We were shock troops at a time in history when ground rules, theories, and the world itself changed so quickly that as Margaret Mead said, our children were the first generation who had nothing practical to learn from their parents' and grandparents' experiences of life (though some of us had children who were vestigially polite enough not to tell us so). Nobody has done the final charting, yet, on full fallout damage to the famous nuclear family, and I'm too shell-shocked to try. But what I *am* up to here is some nonscientific, unsociological, extremely nervous speculations about the view from midlife, some sortings through the experiences of my friends and acquaintances, and as much self-examination as a short person should venture. It's mostly about women because my gender has often determined my perceptions, because most of my friends are women, and because many of my article assignments around the country have involved interviewing women—high school and college students, the elderly, my

3

own generation. My view, I admit, has myopic limitations, shaped as much by middle-class vistas as by middle-aged ones.

Still, the urge to testify persists, a sort of Ancient Mariner syndrome. Marginal survivors often have this compulsion to bear witness, a need to share and maybe even understand a corner of their own experiences in the telling of them. The problems comes in distinguishing information from exhibitionism. "When one no longer knows what to do in order to astonish and survive, one offers one's pudenda to the public gaze," wrote Paul Valéry. And when other people's private matters are at issue (I can change friends' names, but my family is my family), to tell or not to tell is a troubling proposition. My children's blanket endorsement, "Tell it as you see it, Mom," is usually short-sheeted with "We're used to your exaggerations."

Sometimes I've offended, I know, by laughing in the wrong places. I've whined and wept a lot, too, and germinated strange rashes ("You are allergic to yourself," a dermatologist explained), and during one bad time my hair began falling out in rueful bouquets ("You're grieving too much," said yet another skin man).

Like most people my age, I have seen dear friends die of diseases I *know* our parents' generation didn't catch so often or so young. We also got to watch marriages we cared about sicken and die in epidemic numbers—our friends' old alliances, our own. Some went bad and earned their right to decent burial. Others, I suspect, expired from overdoses of contemporaneity. We learned that our food, air, water, and jobs could kill. So could our medicines. But there were quiet heroisms in everyday lives, unexpected beauty, occasional dazzling tenderness.

4

On my own turf, there was one other upheaval on the way to midlife crisis. Five years ago, I began doing what I most feared, desperately wanted, and never before had the nerve to try: I started to write. I was forty-two then and had perfected a lifetime of stalling maneuvers all the way from "I'll do it when the last kid starts kindergarten" to "I'll do it when the last one goes to college." Both excuses implied that I had too many children to total up on a pocket calculator; in fact, there were only two. I'd secretly planned National Book Awards for both; however, one grew up to join the Hare Krishna movement, and you already know too much about what I probably did wrong from the beginning of this sentence. At any rate, when he finally went to what his brethren call Godhead and his sister to college, I finally went to the typewriter.

A great deal of that which has confused me in this life has to do with the disparity between the MGM endings on which I was nurtured, post–"Singing Lady," and the recalcitrant ways of real events. But Louis B. himself couldn't have concocted a frothier, more fantasy-fulfilling payoff for that first effort at the terrifying typewriter. It was a fluke, to be sure, but the middle-aged lady's literary debut—a Chaucerian takeoff on the events of Watergate called "The Waterbury Tales"—received international exposure and generated enough work to keep me going full time ever since. That's how I first began irritating my mother and mother-in-law with endless age revelations and started on what now is the central, stabilizing wonder and daily dread of my life, a habit beyond the help of behavior modification.

But since it was Chaucer who launched me in the first place, I'm about to lean on him to help me begin another late-life first, this book. So I've put a little Middle English on the poem that follows as further introduction to these chapters.

5

Whan that forty with his hot pursuite,
Play happy byrthday to yow on his floote,
And even they who marathon hath wonne
Can no the movyng calendar outronne,
Whan heads that hadde blacke hayr, and blondys
Discovyr in ther mydst som straunge strondes,
Whan dimplyn folks' flesshe with cellulyte,
And troubyl creepyn in on smal crow's feete,
Whan Mothyr Bell hath prynt hir book too smalle,
Whan movyng hands writ HOT FLASSH on youre walle,
Than starts the pilgrymage thru myddle ages,
A tryp the OLDE WYF tel in these pagys.

A WYF was ther biside Mayr Daly's Loope,
She think hir playc were makyn chyckyn soope,
And troubyl on hir door wol fear to knocke,
If wel she lern the DOCTOUR OF Y-SPOCKE.
Quod she, "A good wyf stay at hoom alle daye,"
And "Betty Crockyr Vincit Omnia,"
But though she studye wel the best advyces,
She catch the plague y-clept The Myd-Lyf Crisys.
So whan hir childryn from the nest y-flownne,
She sittyn down to play the Smyth-Corone
And chant her merry tales (with some sad pagys),
Of pilgrymes' travyls thru ther myddl ages,
Of folk who wel koud ryde the streit y-cors,
And folk (lyk hir) that fallen off ther hors.
Of mariages ful vertuous and sounde,
And pilgrymes, truth to tel, that fool y-rounde,
Of childryn bryngyn honours to ther mommyse,
And oother kyds that bryngen hoom ther swamise.
Of mothyrs and of doghtren and all suche,

Of gilt the KNYGHT OF ERHARD ne koud touche,
Of folk I mete, and how it seemed to me,
Of whiche they weren, and of what degree,
The journeye hadde lafs and its travailles,
Of them I beg to tel yow in these tales,
And of the tyme of lyf we folk been inne.
With Olde Mariage wol I bigynne.

Old Valentines,
Old Marriages

My queenly bridal gown has been preserved in pink tissue for twenty-seven years now. The satin shoes that match it are nearly virginal, and so was I the day I teetered down the aisle in them. Last New Year's Eve I broke the old shoes out; they'd come back in style and looked quite contemporary (everyone said so). But the fragile wedding gown will never march again. Though my daughter is nearly old enough to wear it, if Claudia ever chooses to marry, it's not likely that she'll do so wearing my bridal finery. Just as well. That sweeping train and those layers of lace might look strange with her leg warmers and combat boots.

I took the old gown out and stared at it a few days before our latest anniversary. It unnerved the silver-haired groom, who thought I might be plotting one of those renew-the-vows ceremonies you read about . . . where midlife couples get into their ancient wedding attire and summon friends, relatives, and progeny to witness romantic history reenacted. He needn't have feared. I had disinterred my gown because I was thinking about old marriages, wondering what keeps them going, why some stay happy, what my own was *really* like. It was thorny stuff, and I suppose that staring at the gown was my idea of scholarly investigation. (Besides, I'd finished my research into whether, if you listen closely, you can hear your own arteries hardening, and you can't.)

The trouble is, my investigative credentials are tainted by a traitorous streak of romanticism. Not that my heart leaps up for Marabel Morgan, though if such fluffy philosophies keep other people happy and juicy, it's okay with me. But if *I* were dressed in nothing but a garter belt when Shel, my husband, limped home from the office, he'd be right in assuming that once again I'd forgotten to do the laundry. Now that I work full time, he's surprised enough to find dinner ready; a preheated wife would be excessive. Like most middle-aged women—at least the ones I hang out with—I have found neither the burned bra nor the one with flower-shaped cutouts at the nipple to be an emotional or political statement made exactly to my size.

Still, I *do* suffer from virulent attacts of sentimentality, a kind of St. Valentine's dance that compels me to throw an annual February 14th fit of a party. During one February seizure, I rigged out our dog as Cupid. He ate not only his left wing, but all the pink candies on the coffee table and delivered vomited valentines to us for weeks. Another February, I made the ruffle-necked dress of red-and-white heart-patterned fabric that I've worn to my party ever since. (It has an under-the-bosom sash that cries out for Tricia Nixon.) When I also ran up napkins and café curtains in the same material, my husband offered to hang me at the window so that arriving guests could play "Guess Which Is the Hostess and Which Are the Draperies."

I met my wise-ass valentine twenty-nine years ago. I was an eighteen-year-old college freshman; he was twenty-two, an ex-GI senior from Brooklyn whose eyebrows—I marveled—looked just like Tyrone Power's. We "went steady" from the first date, were duly "pinned" and engaged, and I married him two years later only partly because (in the dark garage behind a freshman dorm) he explained, "Sex is an integral part of life." Nobody had ever said "integral" to me before.

Which is not to imply that, in those dear dead days before the word *relationship* was invented, *ours* lacked intellectual substance. An account of our first date survives on a 1949 postcard in my mother's dresser: "Went out with someone WONDERFUL! His name is Sheldon Wax and we talked about Khafke all evening!" Now that we had nailed down Khafke, if not spelling, could eternal vows be far behind? It was an era, of course, when most girls were expected to come back from higher education with a live one. But when *I* came home one month into my freshman year and said I'd fallen in love with Sheldon-from-the-postcard and intended to marry him, my mother counseled gently that I might be rushing things. The way it happened was, she was reading in bed when I broke the news, and her scream for my father brought him running from the floor below. "Milton!" she hollered. *"Speak to her!"* As she would be the first to point out, nobody ever could.

Besides, my friends and I considered ourselves experts about this thing called love. You were in it, we knew, if there was any sexual activity going on (otherwise, nice girls wouldn't be doing that stuff in parked cars), and love meant choosing a lifetime partner and a lifetime silver pattern. Ardelle, a girl in my dorm, threw herself down a flight of stairs one morning to impress her boyfriend with how seriously she, for one, regarded her maidenhead's surrender the previous night. She fell with slow-motion care, though, clutching a duffel bag stuffed with laundry to cushion the impact on her defiled body. But Ardelle had made her point and was triumphantly proclaiming, "I'm pinned!" by dinnertime.

Ardelle-the-leaper and most of my other school friends were married not long after Shel and I were, a ripple effect of weddings that helped sustain my own marriage. Those buffet tables and multicourse dinners in hotels, homes, clubs, and rented halls up and down the East Coast helped balance what was the despair of my domesticity, *The Bride's Budget Book.* Its columns and deficits were matters of ulcerating seriousness for me, particularly the space demanding EXPLANATION that followed each day's accounting. I *should* have answered, "Mind your own damn business," but I never did. (My EXPLANATION for a day our food expenditure had been less than usual was: "Ate gift sardines for dinner.") October 5, 1953's EXPLANATION, "Diaper Service," marked a new expense, a landmark event, and the end of my struggle for monetary equilibrium. It was also the date of my last recorded word in *The Bride's Budget Book,* a wavering "Help!"

You don't have to consult statistics to know what happened to so many of those old unions, the ones that grew out of first-blush college or even high school romances. (Ardelle, the freshman in my dorm who tobogganed down the stairs on her laundry bag, is doing *her* part as statistical fodder; a recent letter announced she was about to take her third husband. Ardelle's lover count has mounted past charting, so either she takes these things less seriously than she used to or she's been living in ranch houses.) But if so many of us have come asunder, and statisticians have scheduled even more for future split, what about those whose stitching appears to be holding up? Is there a common thread?

"It depends on what day you ask me," says my friend Alicia, "but Richard and I have become so accustomed to each other in twenty-three years that our marriage is like any really entrenched habit, and neither of us can imagine ever breaking it. All this stuff I read about 'communicating' doesn't have much to do with us; we both think there's a lot that *shouldn't* be said. But our values are the same, and each of us feels that the other is in some way superior. It makes us *admire* each other. And I trust him absolutely; I can't imagine him betraying me, which makes *me* trustworthy even in moments of weakness. During the rocky periods, when I've felt trapped and isolated, I've always had a sense that if I endured, a better time was ahead. And it usually was. There are probably dozens of reasons Richard and I stay together. But the one that makes people go on loving each other is a total, and marvelous, mystery."

Like Alicia, lots of other "lifers" with whom I've spoken mentioned habit ("We're so *used* to one another") as a prime reason for staying on together. Which might sound fearful, monotonous, bred of inertia and may be all three. It can also mean something quite different. Habits don't have to be bad ones; what about the habit of concern that's nurtured by steady loving, rather than duty? For some lucky people, familiarity breeds content.

I don't know my *own* long-range forecast, but on our last wedding anniversary (the one I spent staring slack-jawed at my wedding gown for clues), I wrote a poem for Shel. His idea of passionate declaration is: "I like you more than life itself," and I wanted to show him that *some* people can express deep feeling with abandon and lyricism. The anniversary poem went:

> The reason our marriage has weathered
> And might even go on nonstop
> Is: When I say, "Notary sojack" . . .
> Your answer is: "Nov shmoz kapop."

No one under forty-five will understand that, but I don't care; let those kids express beauty however they can. (It's even possible, of course, there are people so culturally deprived as to have missed *Smokey Stover* and *Our Boarding House* in the comics of the forties.)

Perhaps Elizabeth Barrett Browning wouldn't have put it that way. But when I ask reasonably contented couples for explanations, they—like I—tend to count the ways with a little less transcendent rapture than Mrs. Browning's "to the ends of being and ideal grace." EBB would have rolled off her chaise at my long-married friend who confessed, "I knew that Phil and I were linked through eternity, because when I asked him to look and tell me if he could *see* the hemorrhoid my doctor said needed surgery, Phil *did* look. And the very same day told me that I was as pretty as on the day we married." Another friend says that her moment of death-do-us-part truth came "when I realized that not even when my children were babies had I ever felt such a rush of tenderness toward another person as the first time I noticed the bald circle that has begun at the back of Seymour's head. I don't know if *he* has spotted it yet, and I won't be the one to tell him, but it's a sort of badge of his vulnerability, his mortality, and I knew when I saw it that I would love him *and* that growing patch of pink skin forever."

Here's what W. H. Auden once wrote about marital longevity: "Like everything which is not the involuntary result of fleeting emotion but the creation of time and will, any marriage, happy or unhappy, is infinitely more interesting and significant than any romance, however passionate." There are those who would quarrel with that poet's credentials as marriage commentator, but I think there's a lot in what he said. Doubtless some people are so good at loving, so flexible, or perhaps just so tricky that they can juggle two worlds: the "romance, however passionate" Auden spoke of and the "interesting and significant" one that is legal. But the daily investment of feeling that goes into some marriages—shared anguish over the kid who causes night sweats or over the endangered job or the hint of illness one is afraid to name (to say nothing of the jokes and triumphs)—makes bonds that can tie up the soul. How those bonds weigh in against what may be missing, and against the heft of a romance that may be delivering flowers, ecstasy, or tension headaches, is different on everybody's scales. But who's to say what kind of passionate bounce is yet left, or only beginning, on some very aging mattresses?

Still, I can only really judge the ticking on my own old mattress and can only address myself to the union that began with a campus decision I once made half of. Doggerel aside, I try to think up reasonable explanations when people ask why this particular brontosaurus is still munching the leaves in the garden of wedlock. And people do ask. Like tour guides so fond of intoning, "If the ravens ever fly away from the Tower, Britain will crumble," or "If the pigeons ever desert St. Mark's Square, Venice will slide into the canal," people tend to say to the Khafke Kid and me, "If you two ever split up, I won't believe in the chances for anybody's marriage." Well, if the ravens deserted London or the pigeons abandoned Venice, I don't know why both countries couldn't just cheerfully anticipate less bird shit.

Sure, we've had some terrific days; whole good years, even. But if Shel and I ever sat down and tried to figure out which of us did what to make this marriage heave, inch, careen, gasp, exalt, despair, lumber, leap, shine, bore, delight, and rattle through twenty-seven years (plus two premarital ones of a little fooling around that any self-respecting modern kid would choke laughing at), we'd probably end in a terrible, terminal battle.

Everyone knows, of course, that merely sticking together isn't proof of the worth of the bond. Consider all the paste-up jobs that *should* have come unglued. The sticky part is trying to figure out if one has achieved worthwhile durability over the years or simply installed wall-to-wall carpeting in a rut.

Maybe worthwhile durability can only be explained by some of the marital milestones. But maybe, instead, the working marriage can only be glimpsed through the sum of its non sequiturs: my friend's recognition of permanence at the feeling a fledgling bald spot evoked, for instance. There isn't a nice mathematical formula for evaluating the cumulative effect of all those isolated moments of marriage-in-progress, nothing that totals it all up neatly. But in the spirit of inquiry, I'm prepared to unleash some non sequiturs of my own. From one old bride, then, a few scenes from a marriage:

- This first is as embarrassing as revealing my tacky behavior at all those valentine parties. When Shel and I were young-marrieds, our way of nailing down the Absolute Truth of each other's questionable statements was to extract the sacred certifying oath "O.M." (As in,

"Do you swear that's true, O.M.?") It stood for "On Our Marriage," and mawkish or not, the swearer knew a lie *guaranteed* divorce ... the worst thing either of us could think of. (That was the early fifties, and we didn't even know anybody who'd ever gotten one.) Before anyone gets too sentimental about the two young innocents who exchanged those soulful O.M.'s, though, it should be noted we also said "O.J." (for orange juice) and "T.P." (for toilet paper). And as life grew more complicated, we lost the habit of swearing on our marriage and at least some of that conviction about the Absolute Efficacy of Absolute Truth.

- Shel was the star pupil of the weekly fatherhood training class he took at the hospital and began carrying pristine shoelaces in his pocket, in case he ever had to tie an umbilical cord in our car. He bathed a practice rubber dolly with such concentration it worked a dent between the Tyrone Power brows, and he learned to toss off words like *amniotic fluid* and *postpartum depression.* But all they wanted to know when he checked me into the hospital was our name—which he'd forgotten. Later, in the clutch of some primordial urge to touch the newborn being held up for his inspection, he cracked his head against the nursery glass that separated father and son with such force (and twice within five minutes) that the thundering sound brought nurses from every station. By the time our daughter was born, two years later, he'd become so cool he didn't even bother to take along shoelaces.

- There wasn't anything in those parenthood courses we took about the kid problems our generation was going to confront later: drugs, dropouts, religions most of us had never heard of. When our own children were small, during the 1962 Cuban Missile Crisis, my most taciturn of husbands actually bundled us all off to Winnipeg, Canada, for a couple of days, an act that may have made us America's first and only refugees. He knew it was crazy, but it was the only way he could think of to "save" his family in case the missiles started flying. Ironic, then, that when disaster *did* hit during the adolescence of that firstborn, no flight to anywhere on earth could have "saved" our son or us. The laughs were hard to come by for a couple of years, but during those years we both learned something about growing up together . . . ready or not.

• But growing up is an uneven process. So that when I say ever-so-casually, "If I should die, Shel, would you marry again?" he knows how to make a face that conveys horror beyond holocaust. (It's hard to distinguish sometimes from the one he makes having sighted liver on his dinner plate.) And when I say in that dangerously thin little voice, "Didn't you think that woman you were talking to for so long at the party tonight was *beautiful?*" I can count on his saying, "I suppose she was presentable," or, "You mean the one with the nose job?"

• He continues to play tennis with me, though I serve with my racket in my right hand and then immediately hurl it into my left hand for the volley. People have told me that no one else in America does that. People also come running to see the switch; they tend to get in our way, too, when they fall on our court laughing.

18

- We hated it when our children grew up and left home.

- We loved it when our children grew up and left home.

- When I began writing a few years ago, the compulsive housekeeper in me disappeared and has never even sent a postcard. I have stopped doing all housework except what the board of health could nail me on. He only panhandles friends and neighbors for food occasionally. He's even learning how to use that funny white thing with gas burners in our kitchen.

- He never bought me a nightgown for its warmth.

- He has been singing "The Carioca" ("Say! Have you seen the carioca? / It's not a fox-trot or a polka") each morning for twenty-seven years. When he sleeps, he raises both legs every few minutes, flutter-kicks, then drops them. He is snoring louder, and lately, there's a dear little whistle in it. I have not killed him.

Well, I warned that all I had to offer was non sequiturs. But if anyone can extract some bit of "how-to" advice from the above, some essence that doth a long and happy marriage make, I'll be the first to stitch it on a sampler.

Perhaps, with the tempering of age, I'll learn to control the romantic reflex and come up with nice solid scientific data on The Living Marriage; with luck, there'll still be life in mine. Meanwhile, I promise never to appear at one of my valentine parties in the old bridal gown that is holding up better than the old bride. Not that I'll ever kick the valentine habit entirely. But next time—with God's help—maybe I'll be able to restrain myself from making lots of little heart-shaped Jell-O molds.

The Twenty-Year Itch: Look Who's Scratching Now

On the other hand, it may not take God's help to limit my production of heart-shaped Jell-O molds for valentine parties. An increasing number of couples I've been inviting for years would only throw them at each other. They would, that is, if it were still possible to invite them to the same social gatherings.

The trouble began in the early seventies, when suddenly a number of women I knew were being abandoned by longtime husbands. It wasn't just that it seemed sudden to *me*; the stricken often reported that the epidemic hit before they'd seen the first symptoms. As with Legionnaires' Disease, nobody had the causes pinned down. But there were certain similarities among the afflicted: most of the marriages had hit the two-decade mark (just as mortgages were getting paid off, people were moving into separate houses); the children of these unions were old enough to be past traumatization and—by national custom—more likely to *give* shock than to receive it.

What many of the fleeing husbands seemed to want was new stereo equipment, fake leather furniture, and (this part made me nervous) very young women with long, straight, glinty hair, center-parted. Some of these guys wanted even more of those center-parted dollies than they did quantities of Naugahyde. As the skeptical matron in a Handelsman *New Yorker* cartoon said to her husband, "I understand you perfectly, Harold. When you say you want to extend your parameters, it means you want floozies."

The newly emancipated were given to trendy mannerisms of speech that unnerved their kids. A lot of them talked "grass," while some even smoked it, and there was a rash of Elliott Gould mustaches. (Styled hair, like safari suits, was popular but optional.)

Separation and divorce figures have doubled in a decade for Americans forty-five and older, and some gloomy experts (working with figures can be depressing) predict it will triple in the next ten years. If they're right, it means that one out of two marriages in the over-forty-five age-group is on the endangered list. And though middle-aged husbands are still applying for exit visas in record numbers, during the past few years I was struck by how many women I knew all over the country were clearing their throats and asking out. Not your basic young runaway wife who, like pregnant, unmarried movie stars, had a sort of pop vogue a few years ago. These women were in their forties and fifties, and what seemed to be the single most arresting feature among them was their lack of rancor. Or passion! It would have been easier to make out what was happening if somebody had turned up the sound a little.

Certainly there are any number of women who are just now summoning the stamina to do what has long been contemplated, and for any number of substantial reasons. Harder to evaluate (though judging anybody's marriage is quintessential arrogance, what the hell—let's press on) are endings with curtain speeches that go something like: "You've been nice, it hasn't been all that bad. And what I want now is another life." The thing that's hard to grasp is not the wrong or right of it, but simply ... where do you get the heft to swing the ax if you're not really *furious*?

To say nothing of where do you get the nerve? Everybody knows that as unattached men grow older, the pool of female "possibilities" increases. But despite well-documented evidence of women's sexual longevity, Ruth Gordon movies, and heady promises from certain fashion magazines, young men are not yet knocking each other unconscious in their rush to the first newly available middle-aged woman. Ripeness may be all, but it is not yet all that popular.

Perhaps the exiting wife may have begun a new career, a fascinating one that is the impetus behind her move. Still, many will line up with the hard-core unemployed or end up serving lunch to somebody else's tiresome husband—though at least now they'll get tipped for it. (In my own worst nightmare version of the fantasy, I am a Saks corset fitter through eternity, and my feet hurt.)

So given the well-publicized perils, it's little wonder that the man who's left behind often appears to be even more devastated than most abandoned women. It's *because* of how tough it can be for the woman alone that her husband can be so shaken; he knows she knows all that ... and is willing to confront it for a whirl at whatever may be out there.

There's often a stunned quality about these men, at least the ones who used to be half a couple at my parties. None was more bewildered, though, than my friend Bernice's husband when Bernice abandoned him for another nice forty-five-year-old lady like herself. "Did *you* know about her? Did you suspect?" he asked her old pals. But like him, none of us ever suspected that there was anything in Bernice's closet except her electric broom. How did her children take it? All three were in college when she took off, and after due consideration, she decided not to tell them her loved one's gender until each kid turned thirty. I guess it was an age she sort of picked out of the air as one which would magically equip them to "handle" it. But something must have made her revise her schedule, because a few of us got Christmas greetings with a picture of Bernice, the "other woman" (how nicely that worn-out term updates in cases like this!), and Bernice's three kids. They were all smiling and looking quite comfortable, if not Waltonishly familial.

I like to think that I'm a kind woman (I like to think I'm voluptuous, too), but though I felt concern for Bernice's husband, I couldn't work up much in the way of compassion for another deserted man I know. I could only remember the complacency with which he'd informed me at one of my parties, "Any woman who expects to hang on to her husband damn well better have a face-lift by the time she's forty." The pronouncement sent me twitching to the bathroom mirror, and just as I'd suspected ... my crow's-feet had turned to pterodactyl tracks.

Not that every rejected spouse is a chauvinist louse like that guy was. One, a neighbor of ours, had been a breakfast tray bringer, supermarket schlepper since he married thirty years ago (all this and faithful, too). Maybe he put his libido into vacuuming; he's addicted to it and goes a little funny if the cleaning woman gets too proprietary with the crevice attachment. Nevertheless, his wife wanted out. "Space!" she wailed. (Can I help it if their windows were open?) "I need SPACE!" She wanted it decorator-furnished, too, and sent her dirty undies home after she'd moved out, for the laundress to deal with.

The night before she left, the couple stayed up till dawn while she explained the reasons divorce was a necessary step in her Human Potentialization. He cried most of the way through it—I'm not sure his pajamas are dry *yet*. However, just as the sun came up, he thought maybe he'd begun to understand at last what had gone wrong. "Tell the truth," he sobbed, "have I been acting too macho?"

My old friend Francesca met me for lunch when she was back in town for a visit, and I paid attention because Francesca is a trustworthy reporter of feelings. And *hers,* she reported, were in prime condition ever since the divorce she'd asked for had become final. Like mine, Francesca's career bloomed late, and we share delight and a little astonishment that we can support ourselves now, though in no one's idea of high style. Anyway, before her marriage expired, it was another of those old specimens people liked to trot out as one last bit of perfection in a world gone putrid. The problem, Francesca said, was that after several decades of alleged perfection, she found herself no longer able to get up and put her clothes on in the morning. That startled me, because Francesca had always been so active I used to think of her as the Energy Czarina. And when she told me she'd become immobilized, I suddenly got the picture of how *much* energy it had taken presenting that confection of a marriage to America after the wedding cake had gone crumby.

The day Francesca and I met for lunch, we picked right up again on the old easy friendship that geography had interrupted. Part of her radiance, she said, was because she had recently been pronounced sound and lifeworthy by the psychiatrist she'd been seeing, and I asked her how both she and the doctor *knew* she was now ready for a clean bill of mental health. "Because when I started with him, I had three goals," she said. "To find work I like, to tell myself the truth, to be able to love someone."

"And you've achieved all that?"

"I have," she said, "although I love somebody who is sort of inappropriate. But it's really okay. I don't want to marry him. As a matter of fact, I don't think I'll ever marry again. And when I feel like sleeping with somebody else, I just do." My smile was wide, generous, and as fraudulent as the day my third-grade rival won the Shirley Temple look-alike contest. Still, I was trying to be professional about data accumulation, and it seemed clear Francesca had done the right thing leaving home. But she's beautiful, talented, employed, and didn't even have to wear thigh-control girdles at a time in history when most women *did;* an example, in short, to be emulated with caution.

Unfortunately, I don't have the credentials to formulate theories from these anecdotes; however, I *have* been engaged in lifelong inquiry. When I was a child, my grandmother and I were this country's leading authorities on "The Romance of Helen Trent," and every day we'd huddle at the radio while the announcer explained that the program was dedicated to proving "what so many women long to prove in their own lives: that because a woman is thirty-five and more, romance in life need not be over, that the romance of youth can extend into middle life and *even beyond*" (emphasis, the announcer's). So, though I probably have my grandmother and Helen Trent to thank for my silly romantic streak, it's also due to them that my research into what the mature woman is up against has been going on since before I collected movie stars' autographed pictures and even before I owned a Charlie McCarthy spoon. I know that if a woman "in middle life and even beyond" *is* looking for romance today, she's probably learned to shut up about it. She'd probably, as I do, agree with Doris Lessing that it's a waste of a life if you hang about just waiting for a man to confer meaning on it. We understand *(don't we?)* that time without a man in it is not waste space. It's just that there's so much else for my moonlight-and-roses-nurtured generation to learn and unlearn.

A divorced woman I met at a party told me that when she's expecting a visit from a "date"—a word that in our middle years embarrassed us both, but we couldn't think of a substitute—her best friend feels compelled to rush over beforehand and check out bathroom corners for hairballs. She sweeps up any she finds and leaves assured that she has enhanced her friend's desirability, to say nothing of remarriage chances. They both *know* it's funny, but the ritual is compulsive, and there's a sort of touching sisterhood in the gesture, even if it owes less to Betty Friedan than Betty Crocker. But look, there was never a more independent woman than Golda Meir, and she was photographed beaming when her Cabinet presented her with a set of dinnerware the day she left office. Doesn't it indicate that you can be a power and still feel okay tossing off the odd kreplach now and then?

For insights into life in general and particularly the life alone, I often look to my unflinchingly honest friend Katie— who embarked upon singleness after a twenty-three-year monogamous marriage. The last time I invited her to dinner I forgot how ardently we *both* believed in Doris Lessing, and I said that though there would be an unattached man in the group, I wasn't sure "anything would come of it."

"It really doesn't matter," Katie said, all poise. "I have friends . . . and I have lovers."

That sounded so sophisticated and contemporary that I was downright envious, and this time I said so. "Well, the truth is," said Katie (who is known not only for honesty, but for what in another era was called "ladylike" ways), "the truth is, I only have one lover." Pause. "And *he's* a pain in the ass."

It has to mean something that every one of the women I'm talking about married young. My generation was dispatched to college as if it were the Husband Super Bowl, and when we didn't know what to do about our feelings—at least our sexual ones—we legalized them. It's well known that Margaret Mead proposed that young couples considering marriage should live together under a contractual two-year legal arrangement after which they'd mutually decide whether to marry or simply dissolve the bond. The idea came a few decades late for most of *us,* but maybe she ought to think up some kind of National Plan for Old Marrieds, too. Maybe there ought to be legal rest stops at, say, the fifteenth or twentieth anniversary, when husbands and wives could elect to separate for a few months and then come back together—no questions asked—and decide whether to cancel or renew. And maybe the rest stop should be mandatory, not elective, so neither partner would feel pressure to deny wanting to try it. I admit the details could get tricky, so I leave it to others to work out things like where one goes, what happens to jobs and to dependents so tactless as to still be hanging around the old nest. Maybe Milton Friedman could work out a plan for the finances. Okay—jokes, jokes. But it does seem that the late-in-marriage breakup has a lot to do with a perhaps only temporary need to taste that world out there. I bet most people would settle back together once they'd had a few licks at it. And it probably all works out a lot cheaper than lawyers and alimony.

The big word today is *choices,* of course. The catch is that despite an explosion of exhortations to make them, nobody has really refined the distinctions between the choices that lead to (watch out: jargon ahead) self-realization or self-destruction. At our age, one ought to get a chance to find out which is which, so we can make an informed decision about whether to crawl back from the edge of the abyss while there's still time or jump into it, hang a few pictures, and discover that the abyss is nicer than home, sweet safe home was. I confess that's a little like asking, "If I make my own bed, do I still get to lie down on percale sheets?" but so what? Even that dummy Goldilocks knew enough to test the mattresses.

It's confusing, but then no age-group has ever gotten a more confusing set of signals. And though we speculate about whether some of our daughters have been pressured into sexual unions because of what they were led to believe "everybody does," what about *us*? Are some of us rushing to leave old roommates because we, too, are feeling pressure in what we hear and read about what the other—um—kids are doing?

I can only offer the slenderest, most empirically fragile data from my wanderings among my peers and my own midlife confusion. I know that when a forty-eight-year-old woman who lives alone and doesn't date says, "I never feel as lonely as when I was married," it's probably lucky she worked up the nerve to do her Nora number. I know from the one who's collecting Seconals now instead of milkglass that boredom has to be better. And I don't think anyone can predict how many of us who walked out will prove to be happier and sounder for it and how many will have been victims of one season's fashion that turned into next year's rummage.

I, for one, will continue to poke around for portents, like an ancient soothsayer looking for signs in the entrails of sheep. What clues are there, for instance, in this postcard from an old friend who married, as I did, before we'd even heard of stretch marks? "Since Stanley let me have the divorce," she writes, "I'm finding my center in Tai Chi, self-exploration, depth-plumbing, seaweed, a soupçon of chemicals, a smorgasbord of sex. What's new with *you?*"

I knew her when she wore dress shields.

The Late-Blooming Affair

There *are* other options besides ripening together in a mellow old marriage or running out on what's gone rotten. One of them—no doubt the word has gotten around—is the affair. But what with the years spent in child-community-and-kitchen craft (and paying attention to Dr. "Can This Marriage Be Saved?" Popnoe), a lot of us didn't discover the possibilities of the double life until we'd been hit by the possibilities of the double chin.

Which doesn't mean the late affair has to be the stuff of farce, a last-chance cavort of aging flesh. Many women say that for them, it has meant lovely erotic discoveries, or rediscoveries. *Some* say the lovely eroticism was discovered because they forgot their assigned places in our youth culture, forgot all that had been carefully learned, and fell astoundingly, extramaritally in love.

And if, in the middle of her life, some beauty falls on a
girl, who turns under its swarm to astonished woman . . .

Those two lines are part of a poem by Mona Van Duyn, who
wasn't suggesting that midlife love has to be of the off-limits
variety. But "in the middle of her life" it can, indeed, happen . . . an explosion that stings, stuns, alters, and makes a
woman terrifyingly vulnerable. What some of us learn—most
astonishingly and painfully of all—is that it can happen not
only when what we had at home was faltering or inadequate,
but *even* when what was familiar was cherished, comfortable,
and loving.

Some religions preach that a knowledge of God, by
whatever name one calls Him or Her, is part of everyone's
unconscious, waiting to be recognized. I don't know about
that, but I suspect that most people, men and women, carry
around some preconscious knowledge of the possibilities of
love, even if the beauty described in that poem never (person-
ally) fell on *them.* Our well-publicized midlife crisis is often a
kind of panic that the beauty may never show up at all. The
fiftyish guy wearing the generous-to-a-fault hairpiece and
dopey expression as he eyes the baby secretaries at a singles
bar, his wife at home memorizing a "You, Too, Can Have Cover
Girl Cleavage" article are easy parody figures. But the yearning toward an ideal of love impels us mortals into funny pos-
tures, unbecoming pursuits, and even less becoming jump
suits.

For some lucky people, beauty was conferred for all time
in marriages that remain impervious to other loves and other
beds. (You don't qualify for either eternal imperviousness *or*
virtue, though, if there has never been a serious challenge by
someone really tempting.) However, if love doesn't ever reveal
itself to us, we aren't above pretending there's no such com-

modity anyway. Which explains why a monogamous woman can hurl herself into one first fling with a man she's not all that crazy about . . . just to get the flavor of the general experience before the taste buds go. Besides, the same women's magazines which used to dish up "Fifty Ways to Stretch Hamburger" as if it were the wildest reaches of self-realization are now running articles with titles like "Your Affair May Help Your Marriage" and "It *Is* Possible to Love Two Men . . . Your Husband and Your Lover." They even offer surveys and statistics that show you don't die of adultery (although the marriage mortality rate seems about fifty-fifty).

Such articles might wind up ending infidelity in America. Take, as analogy, a couple in my neighborhood who are absolutely messianic about the joys of pot smoking. Their children are straight-arrow honor students and spend the few hours when they're not accepting citizenship awards-cum-scholarships begging their parents to—as it were—cut the grass. Last time I visited, the kids had their glazed elders propped up like geriatric rag dolls and were reading reports to them about chromosomal damage and brain erosion. Now you can bet those kids are never going to lie around stoned and grinning foolishly; their parents took the zest out of all that by beating them to it, by approving. And it's probably the same principle with unsanctified sex. Who's going to want to savor forbidden fruit when homemaking magazines are outdoing each other with recipes for Illicit Compote?

Without help from such sources, it's hard enough to keep the domesticity out of adultery. That is, if one takes it up relatively late in life and direct from one's kitchen. I know a long-married woman who—fancying herself in love for the first time—refused to run off with the beloved until they'd spent a little time playing house. She proposed that they rent a trysting place; nothing grand and they'd split expenses. "I thought it was very sensible to do a little part-time tryout first," she said. "Not just sex, but sort of living together a few hours now and then. What really thrilled me, I suppose, was how modern and liberated I felt to have been the one to suggest the arrangement; I'd never even *kissed* anyone except my husband in the whole twenty-eight years I'd been married.

"The trouble was, the day we rendezvoused to go look for our magic love nest, we'd both forgotten our glasses and couldn't make out the ads in the classifieds. We had to drag around to five-and dimes till we found a magnifying glass. I'd never seen Charles in a hat before, and he looked so stolid and husbandly—I mean we felt so hopelessly respectable in spite of our mission that it seemed about as exciting as going to the laundromat together. We both got the picture at the same minute and broke down laughing the first time we rang for a janitor. So we ran away before he even answered and ended up by going for coffee—as usual."

Another woman who is better schooled in home economics than home wrecking tries to get the tiny orchestra in her brain to strike up the world's great love themes, but usually hears instead a long-playing rendition of "Nothing Says Lovin' Like Something from the Oven." And though she spends many blissful hours in her lover's office (he's self-employed), she is neither under the desk nibbling his cherished knees nor frolicking behind the draperies. She attends, instead, to her menus, marketing lists, party invitations, and has even begun bringing along little plastic bags of vegetables—green peppers, radishes, cucumbers—so that if it's going to be a long day's togetherness, she'll have a leg up on that evening's lawfully wedded salad. (She keeps a knife and chopping board in the Other Man's file cabinet.)

Maybe that woman is only acting out long-repressed fantasies, and if her most erotic one turns out to be having a

Cuisinart in two places, why find fault? With all the collections of other women's fantasies we've been reading, it's tough enough to come up with original material of one's own. Not that the double-life fantasy hasn't been a silent partner in lots of good old marriages. What's relatively new for many women is a bite-the-bullet determination to turn fantasy to fait accompli.

Norma, who has been faithful to her husband for the twenty-one years they've been married, confesses that she has been readying what she calls "my adultery underwear wardrobe" for nearly as long. "I'd start fantasizing about some man—for years it was my gynecologist, and for a while a man on my Save Our Trees committee—but nothing ever happened. I used to comfort myself that I probably seemed so unapproachable, so dauntingly wholesome that no one dared kiss Sleeping Beauty. But never mind, I was getting this lingerie wardrobe together just in case there was an aging Prince Charming *somewhere* around who had the balls to break my spell."

Norma's years of "just in case" stockpiling is easy to understand as a variation on wearing holefree underwear in case you're ever in an accident. She probably figured that if she was suddenly struck by unexpected *passion,* why risk being caught wearing elastic that has lost its will to live? But Norma says collecting these flimsies for her fantasy life "wasn't the worst thing I did."

"The worst" was that though her husband was paying for them, he never even got a glimpse of all those nylon numbers she was squirreling away for the phantom lover. "I didn't think that it was ethical," she explains, "to drive two men crazy with the same red girdle. That's right, red girdle. I started collecting the wardrobe when I was so young panty hose hadn't been invented. And the only way I could think of distracting my lover-to-be from those ugly girdle grippers that held my stockings up was to buy this flaming red latex thing with black lace on it."

Norma is readying an impressive collection of Jean Harlow style ecru satin underwear and swears she's going to make her fallen woman debut in those skivvies any day now. (She, too, has seen the "You Can Love Two Men" articles, though she insists that the only thing she reads is *The New Republic.*) "It's a little late for the red girdle," she sighs, "but maybe it's just as well. With my luck, I'd probably have picked a man who would have asked to borrow it."

Several wives I know broke their own long-standing records for monogamy by looking up "the man I *almost* married." "I was the last one left in my book discussion group who hadn't had an affair," one told me, "and so I went stalking the only person in my whole life—other than my husband—who had ever asked me to sleep with him. I did it in cold blood, but I made sure to undress under the covers because the last time he asked me, I was twenty-two years younger and nearly that many pounds lighter. And you know what he said? He said, 'I waited twenty-two years for this, and now I find out you're just like my wife, a closet undresser.'"

A girlhood suitor was my friend Pauline's choice, too. "It seemed the safest way to try it at least once before I die," she said. Pauline was spooning strained apricots into her first grandchild when she told me about her adventure. "Before I married, my idea of being a 'good girl' was to take one more step with each of a succession of boyfriends, and one *less* step than my best friend. So the last boyfriend I had before I married was the one with whom I'd done everything two bodies can manage except actual intercourse. That's why it seemed only the correction of a technicality to call him up thirty years later. And three days after that, we were together in a hotel room."

Pauline wiped some sneezed Junior Apricots off the glasses that hung from a chain on her still-graceful bosom. "I suppose that knowing the man had once wanted to marry me made it okay, in the family, so to speak. After all, if thirty years ago my idea of morality was that I could sleep with the groom-to-be once our wedding invitations were mailed, surely I can be flexible enough today—I mean update my moral code enough to include the man I *could* have married if I'd wanted to. The amazing part is that he actually came all the way to Chicago from Detroit when I called him up, after all this time. I can thank his wife for that. The reason I knew where to reach him is that she's the kind of woman who's secure enough to send Christmas cards to her husband's old girlfriends."

Some late arrivals on the adultery scene are the last people you'd expect to show up at all. One such, wife of a notorious womanizer who began his chasing within weeks of their marriage, had *her* first fling on her fiftieth birthday. (Her husband had forgotten the date, as usual, and anyway, she suspected he'd made previous plans with their dental hygienist.)

I'd always thought of this woman as the essence of primness; there's an aura of "as soon as I finish making popovers, I have to go to choir practice" about her. But she surprised herself and everybody who heard about it by taking to stolen moments—many of which lengthened into days because of her husband's travels—as if to the motel born. She couldn't, in fact, get enough of it and was frank to say so.

But old habits die hard. Such as her lifelong fear of driving and terror of witnessing traffic accidents. Though she is pleased as anything to be rushing off with her unmarried lover for one of their enchanted weekends, she always sits behind him, glued to the backseat so that she can avert her eyes from the perils of the road, even when the drive takes hours.

Another belated secret-lifer I know claims that she has made sensual breakthroughs *no one else* has ever discovered. But the Compleat Sensualist has yet to make one particular advance: she has never gone to an assignation without bringing along her own room freshener for the bathroom. Let joy be uninhibited, unconfined, and lemon-scented.

As for women on whom beauty (imitating Van Duyn's poem) fell in the middle of their lives, some say it has been an insanely happy bombardment. Others I've talked to found disaster had fallen on them, too. Guilt, for one thing, unfashionable, vestigial stuff, but as a life's reflex, easier to despise than to dispense with. And I know women, old-fashioned or not, who gave up their first experience of that beauty the poem describes when disloyalty to a good old mate became unbearable, a Procrustean variation that involved cutting out the heart so one could fit into an old bed again. ("Renunciation is a piercing virtue," wrote Emily Dickinson, a sentiment that will probably go the way of the minuet after my generation.) On the other hand, several women have told me that they made their big renunciatory speeches, finally, not because of "I can't do it to him anymore" feelings for their own husbands, but out of empathy for the lover's wife. "She's just my age," one renouncer explained. "She and I have lived interchangeable lives. I never even borrowed a cup of sugar from anyone, and it was just too late to feel comfortable borrowing somebody's husband."

Whatever the conflicts or rewards of late discovery, a major handicap is often lack of training. One has to get it on-the-job, so to speak, and a lot of us turn out to be more naïve and less experienced than our youngest daughters. So you pick up hints where you can. If you've read Colette's *The Vagabond*, there's instruction in the heroine's remarks about certain women who are "at the age of fatal imprudences." She says, "I have seen satisfied, amorous women in whom, for a few brief and dangerous minutes, the affected ingenue reappears and allows herself girlish tricks which make her rich and heavy flesh quiver. I have shuddered at the lack of awareness of a friend in her forties who, unclothed and all breathless with love, clapped on her head the cap of her lover, a lieutenant of Hussars."

But a Philadelphia woman I know hadn't read Colette, so in the exuberance of her first affair she put on the adored one's Stetson and marched her forty-four-year-old nakedness around the City Line Marriott during one of their regular Thursday afternoon trysts. She was doing an electrifying baton-twirler imitation, she says . . . around the room, over the rumpled bed; she even leaped onto a chair. (She had also drunk more wine than all those years of bologna sandwich lunches in her kitchen had conditioned her to handle.)

When the nude majorette glanced over at her playmate, his grin had jelled into something less than admiring. And though his wife is a woman celebrated for the fact that nobody has ever seen her smile, apparently he needed someone who could be counted on not to do hat tricks, and he returned to his legal lady, presumably forever, including Thursdays. Had he stuck around, he *might* have learned a little about the joys of laughing in bed; no doubt the Philadelphia woman is well rid of her stuffy lover. On the other hand, she'd grown painfully fond of him. And the husband who now gets all of her attention wouldn't notice, she says, if she wore a hat to bed or marched across it leading a drum and bugle corps.

Another hazard of the late start is that one's skills for gauging a potential partner may have only been put to the test once—and not for several decades. So if you're just taking the game up, you can find that you're dangerously out of practice, which is why when some women fall in love, they also fall for lines that ought to be pelted with rotten vegetables.

A first-affair dropout reports that she *knew* the line she fell for ("My wife and I haven't had sex for years, and you're the first woman I've ever loved") was as old as "Twenty-three skiddoo, Chicken Inspector." That's exactly what was so brilliant about it, she says. "I didn't think anyone would have the nerve to try such an antique unless it were true. I also believed he was trying to 'clear the decks' so we could get married, and I took all kinds of risks with my own marriage because *this* was the passion of a lifetime.

"Well, lying to me about his wife was one thing," she says. "Telling me he'd had a vasectomy was quite another. And guess what middle-aged woman found herself pregnant? My husband *has* had a vasectomy, so I couldn't tell him. I couldn't go to our doctor, either, because he'd know it wasn't home-grown. So one nice morning I hauled myself to an abortion clinic, and there I was—forty-two years old and never an unwanted pregnancy in my whole life—waiting to be vacuumed out with a bunch of scared-looking teenagers. I looked around at those poor silly kids, and I knew I was the most childish one there. I also cried the hardest; this one little blonde girl, no more than fifteen, came over and put her arms around me and cried, too. But *her* boyfriend was in the waiting room, and mine—when he heard the news—mumbled something about he thought we were too old to be fertile . . . and took his wife to the Poconos."

Some women say that even after a shattering experience, they found themselves still addicted to the excitement and intensified sense of living once the affair ended. They tend to statements like: "I hated the sneaking around; I was in constant terror of discovery. The trouble is, now that it's over, I sometimes have the feeling my life has stopped happening." (The woman who made that very statement—as well as an apologetic one that the husband to whom she was once again faithful was "very nice, but very boring"—brightened visibly at a compensating thought: "On the other hand, now that my love of the century is over, it's such a *relief* not to have to hold my stomach in all the time!")

The "my husband is boring" confession sometimes sounds like the leitmotif for the late-blooming affair. I've heard it at least as often as *"He's* been playing around all these years—now I get a turn." If the affair turns out badly or causes too much pain, a return to that boredom is sometimes relief enough to augur permanence, and more than one woman renamed boredom tranquillity. ("I wish my husband would have a tiny fling that he gets over fast," a born-again wife says. "We'd be even then; I could yell and kick and get rid of all this guilt I keep reassuring myself I'm too healthy to have.")

Some marriages, postaffair, take on a new solidity . . . a great leap forward after somebody stumbled. In one of these I know about, the wife left clues around so that her husband— much as he resisted—couldn't help discovering what she'd been up to. "I didn't *mean* to be caught, at least not consciously," she says, "and I'm really embarrassed that I have such an unimaginative subconscious it would come up with something as unsubtle as my 'accidentally' leaving a very compromising letter I wrote where my husband was sure to find it. The experience has been traumatic, God knows, but we're closer than we ever were. It's so liberating to be loved, flaws and all, and I'm awed that my husband could survive his own hurt and hang on to me, even trust me again. My lover was very romantic and poetic; he made me feel I'd been brought

41

out of retirement and cast as Isolde. But in the crunch, it turned out I'd been married to the *real* lover of the story for the last twenty-five years."

And just as certain women's magazines—and some of my friends—say, there are marriages that were expiring until somebody breathed new life in the old wife. I've talked to women who swear that for them, infidelity turned out to be as restorative as the Heimlich maneuver. The happiest nouveau adulteress I know is my girlhood friend Greta. She's forty-six, married twenty years, and landed her first job—and first lover—two years ago. "I can't wait to get up in the morning," Greta told me, "and sometimes I can't wait to get *back* to bed the same afternoon, which is one of the advantages of part-time employment! I know it's crazy, but my marriage has never been happier, and I honestly don't know which of my two men I love most—a fact neither of them could handle if he knew it."

Happy as Greta appears to be with her double life, there's another middle-aged woman—a marvelous-looking silver-haired Long Islander—who I would have predicted could manage the late-blooming ménage à trois better than anyone else I've come across. Which shows you what I know!

"Don't you ever feel guilty?" We were sitting in her magazine-cover (very *House & Garden*) pink-and-green bedroom when I asked her that.

"Guilty?" She looked horrified, then amused. "Guilt was the *old* me," she said. "Guilt was the floor-scrubbing, radish-rose-making carrot-curler I *used* to be."

I pressed on, though. Didn't she even feel guilty when her—as they say—boyfriend was in this house, in this very master bedroom (which was a wild guess, but nobody contradicted me) while the unsuspecting master himself was downtown earning the payments for such things?

"Not a bit," said the dashing lady from Long Island. "My children are grown and gone, and I've earned my place in this house after all these years—why should I need anybody's permission to live in it now on my own terms?"

"And if you get caught?"

"Not to worry. I may be new at this, but I'm a quick study. And I like my marriage just fine."

Nevertheless, she's divorced now. Considering what a cool number she had been, it would be easy to feel something as unbecoming as smugness that a have-your-cake-and-eat-it advocate with *that* much confidence had cut off a bigger slice than her husband would swallow. Still, I was grateful. It's pioneers like her who advance the frontiers of research, and she was generous about sharing what went wrong . . . a small detail, really, but prime example of the pitfalls for those short on training.

The lady from Long Island (she's living in reduced circumstances in Queens now) is particularly instructive for "home entertainers" who wish to stay married. What her experience proves is that it's not enough to be able to manage adultery so guiltlessly that you don't get tripped up by teary outbursts and unexplainable nervous behavior. Of course, *everybody*—even the latest of bloomers—knows enough to check afterward for the hat left behind, the giveaway glass, the wrong brand butt in an ashtray.

However, unless one is famous for one's scouring habits, there's mute but damning testimony in the once-too-often raised toilet seat.

Slouching Toward Bettelheim

The raised toilet seat that put the lid on the Long Island lady's marriage wouldn't have caused concern a few years earlier; it wouldn't even have been noticed. Because at that time her sons hadn't gone away, one to college, one to graduate school, one to the Reverend Moon. And even if she *had* managed time for a lover in those days, she'd never have risked his presence in her home . . . no matter how it might have heightened the colorations of that pink-and-green master bedroom. Like many of her peers, she didn't test out her wings—sexually, careerward, culturally—until she became proprietress of what our jargonists are pleased to call the empty nest.

She and I were much too busy being perfect mothers. That's how I met her, in fact, when we were both learning the first thing you had to know during a Preparation for Childbirth class at New York Hospital in 1953. We were twenty-one then, incubating first babies and—in the manner of fresh-from-school, middle-class young women of the period—approached impending motherhood as if they gave grades for it. One studied, as if for an imminent exam, what "the experts" wrote and said, and what they said with thundering unanimity was that well-adjusted children (everyone I knew was mad to have these) required full-time, stay-at-home mothers.

Most of us accepted that and believed in our responsibility to be better at bringing up baby than our own "too rigid" mothers. And what wasn't in Spock wasn't. My fifth-floor neighbor Meg (who beat me to motherhood by three months) explained that the Book was so perfect "bowel movements are even indexed by content, texture, and color." All I had to do was memorize the good pediatrician, do my natural childbirth exercises, and, finally, deliver the goods—panting at the end, not pushing until so instructed. (A rule I didn't read anywhere but invented for the occasion was: "Even if you begin labor, don't leave for the hospital until you've finished washing the venetian blinds." If we'd had more windows in our apartment, our son would probably have been born atop a stepladder, and we could have named him Slats.)

The trouble was, I felt betrayed every time life itself refused to hold still for doctrine. My natural childbirth technique, for instance, was so successful that the Preparation for Childbirth instructor brought her Monday class waddling into my hospital room so those swollen ladies could hear from the Madonna herself how well their exercises and pantings worked in practical application. But the instructor had to be summoned back later to deal with my tears when I couldn't nurse the issue of that exemplary labor. One nurse accused me of something called inverted nipples (it wasn't true, but I wailed anyway); another nurse spoke darkly of my faulty "let-down reflex." So I knew the game was up. Whether or not my nipples were covert, my maternal inadequacies had popped out, and the world would soon discover what by now even the kid himself must be onto—that no matter how I loved, nurtured, and eventually schooled him, no matter that I would buy educational toys, spurn coloring books (because they discourage creativity), permit him to masturbate, and answer every question he had about sex (even before we left the hospital), he *still* might someday land on the couch. And so, dear reader, he did.

If specters of uncertainty crept out at night to scare other young mothers in the huge apartment complex in Queens where I lived back then, we certainly didn't discuss them. Life was a clock-regulated round of child-centered routine—walks, naps, baths, playgrounds, supermarkets—and if you were bored, you swallowed the yawns along with the unbecoming anxieties. The best housekeeper, we all agreed, in my building was expecting her fourth baby in as many years when she turned on the gas and lay down on that immaculate linoleum; neither she nor we ever mentioned it when they brought her back from the hospital, wan but not miscarried.

The only overt rebellion I can remember was the neighbor who bought room-darkening shades for the bedroom her children shared, fed them "dinner" at 4:00 P.M., pulled down those new shades, and declared it was night and bedtime at 4:30. No small voice was raised in protest, and from that day forward she had about three hours more of childfree time than anybody else in all those kid-crammed buildings. I suppose she got the idea from the way people throw a cover over a bird cage, and if her husband only occasionally got to see what he had sired, at least he came home each evening to candlelight dinners that made their marriage what must have been the least diaper-dampened in all of Queens. (One of their early-to-bed babes has become a prominent young physicist; hardly surprising, since he went through the turmoil of the sixties so much better rested than his contemporaries.)

Like most of the young-marrieds in those apartment hives, we saw the obligatory next step in the good life as *lebensraum* in the suburbs. If you could muster the down payment, the backyard and swings were acquired with the second pregnancy. I never knew anyone who questioned that as part of the civilized order of things, any more than I knew anyone who said she didn't want to marry or had fewer than two children without a note from the doctor. Women, *somewhere*, went back to work or school or both, postchildbirth, but nobody we knew did. It might have made you a Bad Mother.

Companionship in those days meant hanging about in a neighbor's driveway or backyard while your kids played with or destroyed each other. You talked schools-to-come, recipes for tonight, maybe even books or local politics. In our whole 500-house, split-levels-in-assorted-colors development, we only had one scandal to exchange: its star the voluptuous young woman whose afternoon absences (she was in a construction shed with a dashing carpenter) were explained to her husband as justification for sitter expenses because she was "taking skating lessons so I can teach it to the children when they're bigger." Her mate thought this goal so worthy that he bought her a pair of figure skates for her birthday, which put the affair on ice while she learned figure eights.

It was not a time in history for human encountering. I don't know what really went on in the dark night of the soul in any of those split-levels around us, any better than I had known the hearts of those other young mothers with whom I'd pushed strollers and swings back in Queens. Nor did anyone know that sometimes *I* cried unprettily when the resident commuter settled in beside me at night. I became expert at the whispered tirade because I was still hot after perfection and didn't want my children to hear that we were a little short on it. But the standard *sotto voce* wail was that men got to choose the kind of work they did, women only got a crack at being the hearthkeeper, and *where was the fairness in that?* My husband didn't know the answer any more than I did; it didn't occur to us there really *was* an answer. He would usually ask if I were premenstrual, which sent me (quietly, quietly) flailing with fury, particularly when true. But those muffled explosions were proof, I knew, that I was an unnatural woman, and better give another dinner party.

We moved to Chicago, right into the middle of the city, in 1960. It was the end of a particular period of innocence in America, a time one teacher has described as the last she remembers when, if a public figure died, the third graders in her class didn't automatically ask, "Who killed him?" My fresh-from-suburbia children didn't even know what the word *divorce* meant, but when they brought grade lists home from their new school, it appeared that nearly half their classmates came not from split-levels, but split homes. Something else, it appeared, had been happening in America. (My son, Paul—age eight then—and I are walking down a Chicago street when he meets his new friend John's mother and is told by her that John is "visiting his father." When the woman moves on, Paul wants to know all about this interesting arrangement, and I carefully explain—ever vigilant against trauma—this thing called divorce to him. But I'm the one who gets the shock when he asks "Was there any mental cruelty involved?" I am still open-mouthed when he defuses his question with "Hey, Mom, what *is* that stuff, anyway?")

"What is that stuff, anyway?" had a lot more ominous implications only a few years later, for my son and other kids all over the country. Only this time, it was "stuff" that you smoked, swallowed, sniffed, even injected. And you didn't ask your parents. I remember being told, at a party in the sixties, that the weakly handsome middle-aged man pontificating on the sofa was someone called Timothy Leary. I hadn't heard the name until then, although that pale-faced pundit affected our lives—and other families—significantly enough so that I've often looked back at the night and wished I'd poisoned his guacamole.

An escapist's fantasy, of course, just like the one I had of fleeing to safety by taking my children back to Quakertown, Pennsylvania, the little rural community where I grew up. I began dreaming about that when kids started dealing their wares openly on Chicago streets and in the private school— another illusory sanctuary—where we'd enrolled our children. But back in Quakertown, when I returned for a class reunion in 1968, nothing had changed. My classmates seemed as sure of eternal verities as their parents had been, and they told me serenely that in the high school, boys weren't permitted side- burns longer than a quarter of an inch, while girls' skirts—in that year of the mini—stayed demurely fixed at knee level. There were no drugs, there would *be* none, and God was in his Pennsylvania Dutch heaven.

The reunion was shortly after the Democratic Conven- tion in Chicago, and many of my former schoolmates congrat- ulated me for living in a city whose mayor and police knew what to do about those long-haired hippies they were chasing out of the parks and gassing on the streets. I didn't tell them that my husband had joined the demonstrators because he thought that business-suited personages had to stand up, too. Nor did I tell my old classmates that my son was a longhair, that he had begun closing us out of his life, and that his behav- ior was beginning to hint of deep trouble. In Quakertown, at that reunion, nobody I talked to had doubts about Vietnam. Oh, someone had once tried to give out a notice of some kind about it near the high school, an old friend said vaguely, but it "wasn't allowed."

What my Quakertown friends told me went against everything I said, back in Chicago, that I believed in, offended my "deepest principles." And how I yearned to come back, crawl in, be part of those placid people.

But the Troubles came to Quakertown, just as they ultimately found their way to almost every backwater in America. They simply took a little longer. Despite those "it won't happen here" predictions, when I revisited my old hometown a few years after that reunion, I saw a small-scale rerun of what I'd once dreamed of fleeing in Chicago. No riots, of course, and nothing politically inspired. But profanity yelled in classrooms, country boys talking about "uppers, downers, and red devils" and as furry as anything Chicago (by this time having a barbering renaissance) had produced. And girls in such abbreviated and often bare-midriffed costumes that an old-time Pennsylvania Dutch teacher said, "I can't hardly concentrate with all those young girls' belly buttons looking at me!" All this—and a graduation marred by shouted vulgarities—within those bucolic borders, in earshot of one of America's first Quaker meetinghouses. Quakertown had backed into the seventies, shoved by rude events that didn't even say, "I beg thy pardon."

In Quakertown, Chicago, and the rest of America there were, of course, plenty of kids who came through. *Most* did. They achieved or didn't, excelled or not, but their behavior had a recognizable historical context. No generation has been spared its bewildering ration of accidents—its children who are ill, damaged, lost—and parents have always grieved and screamed (if silently), "Why us?" My generation, as well, had its standard allotment of the misfortunes our parents, and theirs, could put names to. What was new in our time were some fancy variations custom-tailored for that dreary invention, the nuclear family.

One gets over being a little jealous, if not resentful, of families where the center held, of friends whose kids didn't drop out, who crested the drug wave, survived their political passions or their lack of them, who still come home on legal holidays. But sometimes you hurt for the leftovers: somebody's faded flower child who, though starting to go a little bald now, is still affecting that sort of jaunty, loping stride that once proclaimed his "looseness" and made his tresses bounce. Most of his pals have moved on now; they're in graduate school, maybe, or married, or moving up in executive training programs. He'll ask you for a little cash very politely (it's an even bet that he's had both orthodontia and minor speech therapy), but he is dazed and redolent. And no concern of Mr. Leary's.

Your heart can catch, too, when somebody's beautiful daughter suddenly confronts you late at night as you're pulling out of a restaurant parking lot. She is smiling as goofily as a Miss America contestant and merchandising plastic posies on behalf of yet another yogi. Back wherever home is, well-meaning people probably assure her parents, "Debbie [or Barbara or Michelle] will get sick of that life, you'll see; she'll be back in school [home, working] any day now." Maybe. But those of our children who spent years drifting, hopped up, freaked out, dropped out don't, it seems, get up one morning and announce, "Well, *that's* all over; tomorrow I'm going to Yale."

There is Liza, for instance, whose zwiebacked fingerprints—twenty-two years ago—joined my children's on our kitchen wallpaper. She lives on a commune in England where all the young women, most of them Americans, shave their heads, though male residents do not. Liza visits her Connecticut parents once a year and allows the shorn head to grow into a crew cut as concession to local customs in their conservative neighborhood. Another sop to the old folks at home is that Liza wears clothes during her yearly stay; back on the commune, standard attire is none.

On her last visit, Liza passed around a brochure for parental edification. It explained the wonders of baldness and nudity as levelers that have freed the women of her commune from the bondage of competition and repression. There was a group portrait (I'm sorry Diane Arbus missed it) of nude bald mothers with their nude bald babies, and another photograph of one young woman illustrating *freedom* by doing a show-and-tell genital exhibition for an approving circle of male and female communalists. The text declared that as further aid against inhibition, group sex and partner exchange were encouraged, particularly among married residents. When I saw the brochure, I couldn't help noticing how many fat fellows lived on that commune or rid myself of the ungenerous suspicion that some very marginal males had found a way of gaining more access to naked ladies than Hugh Hefner ever dreamed of.

Liza's parents try not to alienate their daughter with such observations; they don't risk judgments that might cancel their daughter's (and imminent grandchild's) future visits. Not that Liza forsakes the perfection of her chosen life and comes all the way to America just to check in with ma and pa. She is also on official business, entrusted with the mass purchase of a certain brand of long johns. Because, when it gets too cold on the commune for naked freedom, only a special kind of long underwear will do, and *it's* only available in America. Well, everybody ought to have standards and, in Liza's world, one of the big ones is no-shrink dependability.

Her parents have come to terms with the nudity, baldness, sexual grouping, and groping. But given certain parental values, her snuggies-buying jaunt can be as disheartening as raising a kid who won't be caught dead in anything that doesn't come from Bloomingdale's.

Another young woman of whom I am fond came to visit me as she wafted around the country. She didn't drop acid anymore, she told me; she didn't do anything else, either. On her first Chicago visit, when we had overdosed on revelatory exchanges, I remembered that she'd once wanted to be an artist and suggested we go to the Art Institute. "No, no," she said softly. "I have better pictures in my head."

Andy, who is twenty-eight and the son of an old boyfriend, phoned me; he, too, was doing a latter-day Kerouac number—wandering across the country, thinking about what he really wanted to do. He'd been thinking about it for six years, part of the time sitting in a cave in Greece, staring into the water and listening to the philosophizing of a much-revered expatriate called Four-Toed Fogarty. But Andy's funds ran out, and what he thought he'd like to do next was be a writer. That's why he called me. And though he lives on natural foods, he told me he had been harboring a craving for corned beef as pressing as the one he used to have for peyote and "this super hash you could buy in Afghanistan." At the local corned beef emporium, wearing his gigantic bib overalls and a rustic straw hat, Andy looked like the farmer in the deli.

As we broke rye together, he wanted to know how he ought to begin "the writer gig." I gave him the old "a writer writes"; everybody knows it, but what else is there? And since it took me until I was practically doddering to follow the advice myself, nobody believes or fears the truth of it more than I do.

"What do you read?" I asked him. The answer, "I don't,"

wasn't much different from the one I get depressingly often from college students who tell me they are aspiring writers. Andy seemed pretty much even on that score with a lot of the potential competition, though they are younger and part of what school counselors today call the career generation. No Four-Toed Fogartys for these kids; no caves unless there are graduate schools in them.

Andy and I had a hard time sticking to our topic: his future in the world of letters. Like my young friend who claimed there were better pictures in her head than in the Art Institute's famous impressionist collection, little cataracts of boredom clouded Andy's eyes whenever he wasn't itemizing every feeling he has had since the days he evaluated the world through his crib slats, or lecturing about "the trouble with women," "what my father doesn't understand," "the problem with my mother." I told myself that maybe he could shape this effluvium into a novel that will turn out to be his generation's touchstone of shared experience. But I don't think so. Because, after he warmed me with a good-bye hug, after he thanked me for *"really* paying attention, most people don't," his parting shot was: "I'm not, you know, into listening to people."

But Andy's parents, Liza's mother and father, my husband and I were locked into listening. So when the bad times came, we ran about asking psychiatrists, psychologists, social workers, counselors of every persuasion what to do. Why us (and not those *other* inadequate people next door)? There were days I would have accepted anybody's theory, just to neaten things up, tie a name to disaster, and set about the repair work. But nothing we heard felt custom-tailored for our family. However, one social worker told us a story I liked, whether or not it fitted as our very own analogy. It was about a five-year-old child whose parents were wild with anxiety because their adored firstborn had never uttered a word. Suddenly, one morning at the breakfast table, the boy looked up and said accusingly, "THESE EGGS ARE COLD!"

"Darling!" his mother exclaimed. "My darling! Why haven't you ever said anything before?"

"Up till now," said the kid, "everything was okay."

In the lounge of the hospital where our son spent part of his sixteenth year, parents of our general description sized us up as we did them. And just as in those other waiting rooms where we'd made the rounds, you could almost hear the unspoken conjecture: "How did it happen in your house? If you aren't monsters—and funny you don't look it—maybe there's a chance that *I'm* not, either." (Did their kids—coddled beyond coping with the world's cold eggs—fit that social worker's morality tale?)

It is much too tidy—and dishonest, I think—to explain our new-breed casualties as a demonstrable consequence of the barbarous transactions in Southeast Asia or of the drug culture. But a lot of them shared certain vulnerabilities, sensitivities (we *did* want to raise caring people, didn't we?) which at another time in history might have made them sufferers or troubled, but without the climate and chemical means to do themselves in. "Our vines have tender grapes," sang King Solomon. Our vines did, too, and some of the tenderest were simply squashed in the late sixties. Which is not to deny that plenty of them were pretty squishy in the first place, kids who found fashionable outs for some of the most self-indulgent, insensitive behavior any American culture has ever witnessed. One can only testify that it hadn't been foreseen; it wasn't in Dr. Spock's index. Or, as my grandmother used to say, who knew?

If I were a young mother today, I'd understand that a baby's psychic destiny is determined by things a little more complicated than the wrong-way nipples and dud "let-down reflex" that once betrayed me (though today I'd have a new anxiety about whether the PCB levels in my milk might be even more damaging ultimately). I'd suspect that experts come in as many imperfect varieties as mothers do and that a lot of things our chronic labelers rush to classify are capricious, mysterious, and often accidental. Terrific parents and disastrous ones live to applaud valedictorians, Best All-Arounds, Most Outstandings. What some people interpret as success, Richard Cory understood to be failure. And those of us with the cultists, exotic communalists, and all-purpose different-drummer marchers will probably not be able to define the exact dimensions of our successes or failures, either. (But by the conspicuousness of our offspring's costumes and our tendency toward midlife dermatitis ye shall probably know us.)

A very wise friend who is a teacher once said, "I never knew a parent who damaged deliberately, I mean one who said, 'Let's see now, what can I do to foul up this child?' " Some folks, of course, just have natural gifts for it, and despite what my benevolent friend the teacher says, there were undoubtedly card-carrying fiends among us.

But even a monster can care, and besides, it's not always easy to tell which ones are the vampires by the shape of their bicuspids. I learned about that some years ago when my parents were staying at a resort and reported back to Shel and me on the behavior of the people in the next cabana, the late Bela Lugosi (at the time corporeal) and his family. Mother wrote to us describing a terrifying daily scene during which the world's most famous ogre scattered sunbathers as he tore around the pool in frenzied pursuit of his small fleeing son, Bela, Jr.

"Bela! Bela!" implored the vampire. "Come and take your VI-ta-meens!"

Sharing a Son with Krishna

There's something I never told those doctors, the ones back there in the late sixties who were helping us sift through our family rubble to find out What Went Wrong. It just didn't occur to me then to include in the *mea culpa* litany that when Paul was a few months old, I began giving him his midmorning bottle while I watched the Army-McCarthy hearings on TV. And during those sessions, the senator from Wisconsin had only to beam one vulturine sneer into my Early American living room to make my rage well up so powerfully that perhaps the tender babe in my arms sucked it in daily through his bottle and sensed mistakenly that the fury was meant for *him*. I don't think there's much in the literature out of Vienna to link such bileful osmosis with growing up into guruhood; I suspect, though, I would have been just as disconcerted had he turned out to be a Roy Cohn.

Still, I didn't raise my son to be a "Krishna." It isn't, as they say, work for a Jewish boy. But Paul—who's twenty-five—has been in the International Society for Krishna Consciousness five years (a time period the relentlessly middle-class voice in my head persists in tabulating as "By now he could have his master's degree"), so it's beginning to look like steady work.

How do you get a fix on the precise moment a bad time began? Doris Lessing wrote in *The Four-Gated City*: "When a bad time starts, it is as if on a smooth green lawn a toad appears; as if a clear river suddenly floats down a corpse. Before the appearance of the toad, the corpse, one could not imagine the lawn as anything but delightful, the river as fresh. But lawns can always admit toads, and rivers corpses." Probably the toad had been squatting in our crabgrass and the corpse afloat in our wading pool way back in the split-level days, years before we were forced to acknowledge their rude presences; maybe our neighbors had long been holding their noses and pointing. We never noticed. But it was clear by Paul's midteens that something had gone ugly and wrong for that gentle, open boy—the reader, the kid with all the hobbies—who used to be as quick with a joke as to throw his arms around you. When the bad time dug in, no one could penetrate his icy anger—at us, school, the war. At himself. Nor could we pierce his despair and, what was worse, his terrible loneliness.

Things got worse. He moved from marijuana to hallucinogens, and we began an apprenticeship to grief, an acquaintance with police reports and emergency rooms (if no one on duty speaks English, it's hard to find out whether the pumpee behind closed doors is still breathing). We witnessed the utilitarian decor of a padded cell when Paul spent most of his sixteenth birthday in one because somebody had gifted him with the adulterated LSD that sent him raving out of control on the street and into a patrol wagon. (That night in the hospital parking lot, I heard a woman scream crazily; then Shel put his arm around me, and I knew who the crazy lady was.)

He recovered by morning, but there were more frightening incidents, and the psychiatrist Paul was seeing recommended hospitalization, in a private place, with daily therapy. We wept and agonized and ultimately delivered up the furious body. Once he'd been admitted, the psychological tests showed him to be nonpsychotic; his doctor pointed out that it would also be nice if he got to be seventeen. Looking back, I don't know if the hospital was the right thing. We found out later that during his confinement he continued taking LSD and mescaline, largess from visitors and other patients. If anyone on the staff noticed, nobody ever mentioned it to us. He stopped, finally, the way most hallucinogen users of that era did—after flashbacks so terrifying he never wanted to live through them again.

After the hospital, Paul did his last two years of high school in one, but dropped out of college after two months. (He'd taken his SATs a few weeks before the hospital, and his verbal scores had been about as high as you could get; so—it turned out—was he when he took the tests.) He said he'd had enough of "living like a parasite." Then he dropped his doctor and hit the road. Shel and I were having dinner at some friends' house when his sister phoned nearly incoherent with weeping to say he'd just taken off—alone, penniless, his gear stuffed into an old striped pillowcase.

We heard nothing from him for months; it was the summer the newspapers were full of stories about a basement in Texas where the tortured bodies of missing teenagers had been discovered. Our missing teenager, though, reappeared in the fall, unannounced and very subdued. Somewhere out there on the road he'd kicked the anger as well as the last of the drugs, and for the first time in years, he told us that he loved us. I sensed—and he hinted—that something had happened during his wanderings that had terrified him. One night after dinner, when the others had left the table, he put his hand over mine, and I knew he wanted to talk about it. But I turned away, afraid I'd never get rid of what he might tell me.

On the Jewish High Holy Days he surprised me by going along to services (an outing he'd always resisted), looking gaunt, wild-haired, and sad in his one respectable jacket bought for college interviews the autumn before. I wanted the sermon to inspire us somehow, as feeble a salvation fantasy as all my others. Although the world was exploding that year with campus confrontations, city riots, moral crises, the rabbi confined the heat of his rhetorical passion to beating around the burning bush. Afterward Paul didn't comment, and I didn't dare.

He grew quieter every day, alarmed us with his fasting. I began finding books about Eastern religions lying all over the house, and long after the rest of us had gone to bed, I'd hear him pacing downstairs, sometimes until dawn. Then he moved out of our Chicago home and into a place he'd started visiting, the Krishna movement's temple in suburban Evanston.

In those last three or four years before Paul joined up, even the ringing of our phone when he wasn't home caused a clutch of Pavlovian fear. Our expectations had narrowed to hoping he'd make it from birthday to birthday. So that while hearing a son has declared for a life of Eastern-style asceticism hardly produces parental delight, how you respond depends on where you've been. For us, though we protested strenuously, a sort of relief tempered the basic repugnance. If the sect sounded weird—and it did—at least it held out a small hope of safety, structure, companionship. Shel and I had both tried most of the conventional ways of working out all that

Failed Parenthood Guilt we'd been reeling around with. We grieved; we blamed ourselves. But even the most dedicated self-flagellant's arm can get tired. Besides, I'd decided to use *mine* to write, that thing I'd had a lifetime's fear of trying and didn't risk until Paul climbed into Krishna's chariot.

At the bottom of the bad time, if we were guilty of any child abuse, it was our self-protective neglect of the one who *wasn't* causing trouble. While Paul was in the hospital, we simply didn't allow ourselves to see how stiff with pain Claudia was when she'd come home from school on a day someone in her eighth-grade class had said, "Hey, is it true your brother's crazy?" She'd always been protective toward Paul, alternately devastated and exasperated by his behavior. And when he took up with Krishna, her worst fear was that somebody might hurt him by laughing at his shaved head and peculiar costume. But she's tough as well as tender, and she made it clear to us that she wasn't accepting transferred expectations. Then she beat it out of danger by winning a year-early college acceptance far from home.

When things went so spectacularly wrong with us, people heard about it. Our privacy was blown and we lost our lease on *Good Housekeeping* family perfection. Losing *that* turned out to be a liberation. Which is why it was strange we could still muster anything as frivolous as embarrassment. Nevertheless, for months after he joined, we avoided all downtown areas where Paul and his Krishna colleagues might be doing their brand of street theater—singing the Hare Krishna mantra while they did an accompanying jig. It wasn't the choreography or lyrics I minded (the tune is so grabby I find myself humming it around the house when I'm not working on hits from the forties). What I was afraid to see was the ecstatic glaze on my son's face that I'd seen on other kids before. I simply wasn't ready for beatitude on State Street.

All we knew about the movement was some of the rules: no meat, eggs, fish, drugs, nor any stimulants such as tea, coffee, liquor, or "illicit" sex (the licit variety was limited to married couples and only in the postprayer quest of "more children for Krishna"). Paul told us on the phone that we were to address him by the new "spiritual name" he had been given, Pundarika dasa, and that he'd been made a *brahmachari,* or celibate student. I also got the news that when I grew old, Paul's responsibility as a proper son-in-the-faith would be to look after me. I could see myself in my dotage, wandering the world in my holy son's wake; it didn't seem likely I'd be ordering my hair shirts on a Saks charge.

We found out more when we ran out of excuses and finally accepted an invitation to his temple's "open house." It's a standard Sunday event, heavy on ceremony and sermonizing, and the devotees knock themselves out for it with a big feast of *prasadam,* the Hindu-style vegetarian fare which they insist bestows spiritual uplift by the very tasting. One gorgeous young woman, a saried Ali McGraw, told me that when the rabbi her Ohio family had sent to persuade her homeward tasted it, he said, "Listen, if I didn't have so many commitments, I'd join up myself." A young man educated in Roman Catholic schools informed us that by chanting Krishna's name "and thereby acknowledging his presence in like every human heart," one could end the weary cycle of birth and rebirth and spend eternity in the movement's version of heaven. He explained karmic destiny, the folly of "sense gratification and gross material pursuits" (here the visiting mother standing next to me slipped off her jeweled bracelet and slid it into her purse), given life's transience.

But who could concentrate on fine points of theology? I was girding for the first glimpse of our eldest with shaved head, wispy ponytail, and one of those Indian dhotis Krishna males wear. Their appearance and dress made me cringe, even though I told myself that if Jesus, Moses, Mohammed, or Buddha showed up among us today, he probably wouldn't be wearing a leisure suit. It turned out that Pundarika-alias-Paul was delayed at the laundromat; as newest recruit he was his brethren's dhoti keeper, and by the time he arrived, my eye had accommodated to guru couture. Not that adjustment was a snap. Though I tried to chant the mantra, the part that goes "Hare Rama, Hare Rama" churned in my head as "Hare Rama, I'm the mama!"

In time, though, I came to tolerate and even have a sneaky fondness for those occasional Sunday visits. There's a lot of joyous singing and dancing, with the devotees' own children hurling themselves into the action as rapturously as my kids did when they were little and used to imitate the tribal dances on Dick Clark's "American Bandstand" TV show. Sometimes, at the temple, small hands would pull me into a sort of Krishna-round-the-rosy; sometimes I'd dare transcendental takeoff with a sort of midlife jigalong of my own.

We even went to a Krishna wedding, practice in case we ever had to attend one as parents of the groom. It was very colorful and gay, the young bride adorned with rose petals, beauty marks, and a filmy new sari, the groom amicable, if gawky. Despite their Hindu finery, there was a recalcitrant midwesternness about the newlyweds; the bride's parents had flown in from Iowa that very morning. Her father's maroon jacket stood out among all those saffron robes as if a marauding tribesman had invaded ancient India; her mother, neatly pink-suited, had ironed the bridal sari just before the ceremony. "The last thing of Lauri's—I mean Radakalindi's—I ironed before *that*," she told me, "was her pompom girl outfit."

Even though Shel and I were beginning to feel reasonably

relaxed visiting the Evanston temple, it made me as nervous as the street dancing once did when I'd ask Paul how he was and he'd answer, "I'm blissful." Blissful indeed! But as the months passed, he was clearly feeling better about himself than he had in years. He'd lost his worst affliction—loneliness—and now that it had been given a Brahmanical context, he could accept the intelligence that used to make him feel "different." (No matter what airport I'm in, if I tell the Krishna-wares seller that my son, Pundarika, is one of the flock, I'm likely to hear, "I know *him*. He's the scholar!")

Just as he had taught himself to read when he was three, he began to teach himself Sanskrit. Later he traveled around the country, spreading the word. He was always hoarse, red-eyed from the 4:00 A.M. reveille that starts every devotee's work-pray day, and usually too busy to spend time with us. When he did, his conversational style was the harangue. Once his sister cried and said, "You never ask about *my* life!" He explained it was her eternal soul that concerned him, and a few days later he left some special yogurt in our mailbox and an Indian sweetball for that fallen soul our dog.

If the downtown dancing and "I'm blissful" line discomfited, they were better than past pain. There was still a pang or two left, though, like on the dark cold night Shel and I bumped into Paul in a high-crime area of Chicago, far from his suburban temple. He was alone, trying to sell incense—his sneakers (leather is verboten) were ice-caked, his hands (even swamis lose gloves) raw. He'd been spit on, and someone had thrown most of his merchandise on the street. So there was pain again, yes. But maybe there was less despair for him in it than pity for myself.

He'd been living in the movement's centers around the country for two years or so when I dropped in unexpectedly at a temple he was visiting and found him lecturing a crowd of nearly one-hundred devotees and visitors, explaining doctrine, quoting scripture first in Sanskrit (the Krishna Consciousness philosophy is based on Sanskrit writings of the ancient Vedas) and then in English. I horrified myself by bursting into laughter at a joke he made—it took me by surprise that mystics deliver one-liners—and saw him struggle to control the invading smile of sinful pride.

Laughter helped. Shel and I weren't mocking our son's beliefs or the movement, but sometimes we had glimpses of ourselves as characters in some parody of the American family—the Louds-gone-Vedic. One night, following a temple visit, I woke my sleeping mate and said, "What are we going to do if Paul marries and sends his kids to *gurukula*?"

"What the hell is that?" he moaned.

"You know, one of those boarding schools they run for their own kids. They're called *gurukula*. What are you going to do when they tell you they're sending your own first grandchild to one of those places?"

"I'll pretend," he said, "they told me Boola Boola."

That day at the temple, I'd seen Shel turn red with frustration as Paul proselytized with hard-sell stories of Krishna's wondrous feats. And when our son told his father-the-editor that the sect's magazine, *Back to Godhead,* was going to be "bigger than *Time* or *Newsweek* someday," Shel reddened again and muttered, "Catchy title." Not that he'd lost the old habit of tenderness toward the yogi-robed son who sat there exhorting him. But ascetics don't like it if you hug or kiss them, so sometimes you hide behind a joke. Well, where is it written that a saint can't have the added travail of wise-guy parents?

Will Durant must have been prescient when he predicted in 1935 that a day would come when the East would begin to deify science and the technology-weary children of the West would "forge for themselves another mystic faith to give them courage in the face of hunger, cruelty, injustice and death." Just as Durant foresaw, at the very time India began venerating nuclear godhead, American students crowded seminars in Eastern philosophies, while Asian saviors, boy sages, and hairy-eared swamis crisscrossed the States with mystical messages.

Visiting the Krishna movement's temples around the country, living for nearly a week at the temple-school in Texas, I began to know other people's kids who—like my son—had responded to one of those messages. Many of them were bright and personable—zealots, but gentle ones. Some were casualties: dropouts and degree holders, ex-druggies, ex-straights. The kids I talked to spanned all religious backgrounds, casual and observant, and as many seemed to come from conservative as from "permissive" families. Some had been disowned, some did the disowning, others kept in close touch.

What's hard to confront is that many of our children have found something in sects such as this one that they couldn't seem to grab onto elsewhere. Purpose? Limits? Structure? A rationale for what most of them call "a hellish world"? I don't know, just as I don't know whether what went wrong in Paul's earlier life was homemade or an accident of history, genes, mutation, susceptibility. Or all the above. But we could see, as he could, that our son had found a way to keep from falling off the end of the world. And though there is one face we have stopped looking for at the Thanksgiving table, we are still a family, if a fragile one.

Shel's parents and mine have come further in understanding than we have, considering that the experience of most of their generation was that one's children more or less shaped up as expected. It is unsettling, after all, that the grandson they once took to duck ponds now looks and sounds as if he'd grown up along the Ganges. My mother says he lectures her "like Abelard"; my father says he doesn't care much for Paul's tailor. But all four grandparents observe his birthdays, exchange letters with him, pay temple visits, and refrain from asking if he's *really* getting enough protein till they've hit him with a peppy "Hare Krishna!"

I once suggested to our parents that they could field unwelcome inquiries with: "Paul? He spends so much time in the temple, we hardly see him." If it implied that out there in Illinois a rabbi was in the making, maybe it wasn't so misleading. The time I'd heard him lecturing "the congregation" in English, then quoting in Sanskrit, he sounded like the quintessential Talmudist. Perhaps what we have here is simply a case of skewed tribal memory.

He spent his fourth year of devoteehood living in India, traveling from temple to temple. We got occasional letters from him that were chatty, affectionate, and so serene that we went on with our lives lulled by a sense of his well-being. So it was a shock when a letter not meant for our eyes was forwarded on to us. It had been written by a visitor to the little temple 100 miles from New Delhi where Paul had gone, and it said of our son: "Pundarika is dirt poor, clean but in tatters. I met him on the road after he had walked miles in the hot sun, despite dysentery and a skin eruption, to renew his visa, and he was unable to afford the rickshaw fare of a few cents or a cold drink." So the sleepless nights began all over again, along with frantic attempts to phone, but the lines were down between Delhi and that little village where our holy man was living. Plunged back into the bad old days, I was surprised—and furious—that I could grieve over him again. I felt cheated to find myself still so reachable.

There was some comfort, though, further on in the letter: "What comes through clearly is that this is no bunch of brainwashed freaks; they have voluntarily chosen their way of life as a path of personal salvation. Many of them are highly intelligent and the sweetest, gentlest people I have met in a long time. Pundarika is totally devoted, expects to do this the rest of his life, seems to have made peace with himself. He is a scholar, not a parrot, and I like him enormously."

When Paul and Claudia were small, I used to say smugly, "I want them to grow up thinking for themselves." What I didn't know I really meant was "think for themselves as long as I can stand their choices" (and not be embarrassed to talk about them at class reunions). Still, Shel and I do the work we chose, so we ought to be able—I tell myself—to allow the same to our progeny, as long as what they do is legal, fulfilling to them, nondamaging to others. A lot of the time I believe that. (And all of the time I believe that bit about freedom of religion in the First Amendment, even religions far from first choice for one's own firstborn.)

We finally got a call through to Paul in India. He assured us that his dysentery was mild ("Everyone gets it"), that he wasn't too impoverished to spend a few cents, but "too tight," and that he was thriving. A month later, on that good old Vedic-Kosher holiday Mother's Day, I got a call just like regulation moms all over America. Unable to extend his Indian visa for another year, Paul had just landed in New York. He flew to Chicago next day and, for a few weeks, stayed in our house. It was the first time he'd lived with us in four years. He was taller, not nearly so thin, with an annoying Indian lilt to his speech he soon abandoned, a new dignity he didn't mind surrendering for a laugh, and two parasitic infections it took months to civilize.

In India, he'd begun writing while he was editing the movement's newspaper. His goal was 1,000 words a day, he said in a letter, and startled us by asking that we send him a copy of *The Elements of Style* and other books about writing. Now, at home, he was devouring newspapers and magazines, and insatiable for conversation about American politics. Not that, living among his family of infidels, he cheated on the rituals of his persuasion. He did his own cooking in his own untainted pots, while the monotone of his chanting became the Muzak of our house (and made me appreciate his father's daily rendition of "The Carioca"). But the hard-sell proselytizing had ended; the swami even started jogging! And he'd grin sometimes and refer to himself as the Fanatic.

The first morning home, Paul went off with his father to Shel's office, wanting to use some reference material in the library there for an article he was going to write. I hid at an upstairs window and watched them head down the street together, gray-haired father casually dressed, his papers in a canvas tote, son shorn and Gandhi-robed, looking very official with an elegant borrowed briefcase. They were chatting easily, as if they did this *every* morning, and both seemed innocently unaware of the stares from passersby that confirmed them as an odd, if contemporary, couple.

Pundarika went back to live at the Evanston temple, as he once had before he'd gone to India. He was taking photographs (an old predrug enthusiasm) and continuing to write. When his first effort appeared in an Indian periodical, he was distraught that he'd been edited without consultation. "It's lost its flow!" he fumed as untranscendentally as I do when I yell my standard "They've made my piece sound like a maniac's telegram!" Then he got a chance to do unto writers as he'd been done to when he was summoned to the West Coast as an editor for the movement's monthly magazine.

Paul told us he had come to realize that his religion "doesn't demand that you negate God-given talents, but rather that they be used in service of the Supreme." He said that maybe he enjoyed his new work so much because it agreed with his karmic destiny—what with his father's being an editor and his mother a writer.

Sometimes, in the middle of the night, Shel and I discussed the new developments. Thank God (or Lord Krishna), we told each other, Pundarika/Paul seemed productive and happy. It made us happy, too. But we didn't take it to mean that our son had gone into the family business.

Guilt-Edged Insecurities

When that Krishna personage was still lolling about in his stroller disguised as an American baby, there was a lot of talk about guilt among the park bench mothers I hung out with. And we pretty much settled the issue by agreeing that our kids weren't going to have any. Though the aspiration occasionally worked out so well that some of those fifties babes made Lizzie Borden look overly concerned with parental feelings, most of them seem to be nice, caring people who have, indeed, made it into adulthood without bringing along their own private prosecutors.

But even if those healthy kids have psyches that are suitable for framing, they have come to maturity otherwise deprived. My generation acquired what John Updike calls "guilt gems," and we got them from master cutters. Such jewels can weigh heavily, it's true, yet part of our legacy has been the sort of funny, awful guilt stories our kids may never know about firsthand. Poor unneurotic disinheriteds! They'll have to go through life never having known the likes of Shirley and her mother, for instance.

Such specimens as Shirl and her mom will soon be as extinct as the giant Shasta ground sloth, whose 40,000-year-old droppings ("endangered feces," according to an Iowa newsman) are being excavated from caves as clues to animal history. Shirley, at fifty-one, is considerably younger than the giant sloth; in fact, she could be called a battered child. Not that she was ever physically beaten, but her id and soul have been bruised beyond recognition by a mother who—to steal a Saki description—was as full of herself as an egg. It didn't leave any room for her only child, Shirl, who through a dismal adolescence, two cursed marriages, and various financial disasters always could count on her mother's refusal to lift a finger in aid. She probably *couldn't* lift them; the woman's hands were nearly paralyzed by diamonds.

Battered children often show excessive concern for the well-being of the very parent who brutalizes them. It's probably a keep-the-beast-happy survival technique, and Shirley, too, was obsessed with winning the approval of *her* brutalizing parent. The old lady, a famous beauty, had landscaped her life with millionaire husbands in successive bloom. But her most impressive achievement was the amount of guilt she'd planted in poor Shirley.

One day, Mama was zapped in her Roman bath by a sudden and mysterious affliction. She was rushed to intensive care and diagnosed as beyond the help of medical science, or even Tiffany's. Shirley went wild. She glued herself to her unconscious mother's bedside, keeping a round-the-clock vigil. What *really* kept her there, she told friends later, was the desperate hope that the dying woman would wipe out a lifetime's coldness and injustice with one gorgeous gesture of graveside remorse.

So naturally Shirley was pretty excited when at last Mama flicked an eye open and painfully signaled her need to convey a terminal sentiment. "Pennn-cil!" she gasped. "Paaaper!" Then she struggled heroically to scratch out what Shirley *knew* would be one last (one first!) loving maternal message. "Shirley," the note said, "WERE YOU HERE YESTERDAY?"

I myself have one of this country's noteworthy guilt aptitudes, and to have achieved prominence in *my* age-group, you have to be more than a casual forehead smiter. Our generation was probably the last one to buy wholesale an obligation to live out parental expectation, and the first to try not to unload all of ours on our own kids. It was pretty confusing for all three generations, and as usual, a lot of the experts changed rules as fast as you could learn the latest jargon. The guy I wish I'd met in my formative years is a psychologist I heard being interviewed about his amazing success record in helping chronic pain sufferers. His standard advice to his clients is: each time you pass a mirror, glance at yourself and holler, "Not guilty!" However, it's too late for me to use the technique; my image would yell back a list of indictable offenses. And right up there near the top of the list would be my 1964 co-chairpersonship of something called Chicago Volunteers for Lyndon Johnson (because he said Asian boys should fight Asian wars). It is megalomania at its worst, yet I'll go to my grave believing that I single-handedly gave this country that president and that war. But you can't always stay in the white heat of global culpability, which is why I depend on the exertions of some of my friends (like dear old Shirley), people who are good enough to take on at least a little of the earth's total guilt consignment.

Joyce, a distant cousin, does *her* bit with anxiety attacks for which psychiatrists write in to get tickets. Over the years, Joyce has been analyzed and est-ed, she has screamed primally, boxed herself into orgone claustrophobia, Rolfed, and—in a young neighbor's tire-taped, duckie-decorated backyard wading pool—reenacted her own birth, none of which changed anything or loosened guilt's grip by a finger. I don't dare tell her such rigors are hopeless, considering one detail I remember from our childhood and those countless nights I used to "sleep over" at Cousin Joyce's house. "Good night, Mommy," I hear little Joyce chirp brightly to Aunt Louise. "See you in the morning!" And the answer never varied till the day Joyce left for college: a wan, nearly inaudible, "I—hope—so."

Bruno Bettelheim once tried to give the stock guilt-dispensing Jewish mother equal time by ghosting a journal allegedly written by Mrs. Portnoy. Perhaps after she'd had a chance to tell it her way, Mrs. Portnoy's complaint should have ended the genre; perhaps American letters will collapse under the weight of one more mother-son anecdote. But since my generation was the one dedicated to guilt eradication, don't we have some historical obligation to pass around the remaining stories while they last? Anyway, the following one doesn't really count, because I promised Shel (who is fifty-one) that I'd never repeat this long-distance exchange between him and an unidentified woman in Florida.

SHEL: How are you, Mother?
UNIDENTIFIED FLORIDIAN: Not well.
SHEL: What's the trouble?
U.F.: Well, I have these terrible pains in my back.

SHEL: Gee, that's too bad, Mom. When did they start?
U.F.: When you were born, Sheldon.

Childbirth, of course, is prime guilt grist. Norman is fifty-four and a distinguished academic, but he wouldn't know it was Sunday unless his widowed mother recounted her Day of Rest specialty, the wondrous story of how Normie broke her pelvis on his rude way into the world. Another way he learns it's Sunday is that's when he picks up his mother and brings her home for the afternoon (during which she pursues her hobby of watching him type up his scholarly notes) and for dinner. One recent Sunday morning, when he phoned at eleven as usual, his standard "I'll come by for you at twelve-thirty, Mother," was met by troubling silence. "Mother, did you hear me?" said Norman. "Mother, are you *there*?"

A faint voice finally advised him to hold on while she tracked down a pencil. "I'd better write the time down, Normie. It's so *long* from now."

In some middle-aged sons, guilt takes interesting detours. My mother's pal Mrs. Gotkin has three balding "boys," a plastic surgeon, a proctologist, and a hairdresser. Though she pronounces them "all high-grade and perfect," Mrs. G. wouldn't dream of complaining about the evident problems she is having making it on widow's benefits or confessing that the three high-grade sons are as slow to send a small helping check as they are a Mother's Day geranium. A tiger for "keeping up" on things contemporary, Mrs. Gotkin said that she believes her sons to be suffering from "guilt complexities." She explained that as is usual in such matters, the trouble goes back to their innocent childhoods, a time when she worked in the family grocery store all day, then rushed home to her domestic and maternal chores. "I should have realized what I was doing to them," she said. "Back then, you see, we didn't know about such things. But even when my boys were little, it made them heartsick to see their mama working so hard. And to *this very day,* the second I get down on my knees to scrub a floor, they have to leave the room!"

I've seen people try to turn the tables and make their parents feel guilty, though I never knew anyone who got away with it. One friend, weary of his mother's endless imperious commands, erupted with, "For God's sake, Mom; couldn't you just *once* say please?" *"A mother,"* she informed him, "doesn't *have* to." Another confident matriarch consented to weekly dinner at her son's house but showed her opinion of her daughter-in-law's housekeeping by refusing to sit down—that is, *all* the way down—on the family toilet seat. Her weekly demonstration of implacable standards meant that whoever followed Grandma into the bathroom was confronted with such puddling that one Sunday, her descendants all rebelled. "I swear I *always* wash the seat with ammonia, Mom; it's perfectly safe to sit," said her daughter-in-law, and reproached herself all week afterward that the older woman's feelings had been damaged. That is until the following Sunday, when her mother-in-law sailed in triumphantly with an institution-sized carton of Sani-Johnny Seat Covers clutched to her Persian lamb.

After Shel's paternal grandmother died, Grandpa Wax's grown children worried about the elderly gentleman's adjustment to going on alone. When repeated phone calls to their father went unanswered one Sunday morning, sons and daughter rushed to Grandpa's apartment in alarm. "I *knew* we shouldn't have allowed him to live alone," said one. "It's all my fault!" cried another. But when they burst in, Grandpa was cooking a nice pot of soup and singing his favorite made-up song ("Evabody, evabody, evabody goes to the country . . .

buuut me!") "Damn it all, Dad," sputtered his eldest, "why haven't you answered the phone all morning?" "You want to talk to *me*, I am here," said Grandpa. "You want to talk on the *phone*, call an operator."

God knows, guilt isn't an exclusive Jewish commodity, though many of my people have the true calling for it. So when I heard that a young man who billed himself as an "alternative" rabbi was giving a Rosh Hashanah sermon, I rushed to check it out, in case he had some new approaches to old guilts. But his plunge-necked body shirt, gold neck chains, and yarmulke-topped Afro so distracted me that I missed the message entirely. And though a friend in California audited another new-breed cleric's talk on "Yom Kippur and Guilt," she left when the part about his problems with tennis elbow went on too long, so perhaps guidance must come from secular, or at least traditional, quarters.

There is an aristocratic dowager, pillar of church and community, who is famous for her hauteur and reserve. On her seventy-fifth birthday, she gathered the family round for important news. "There is something I have been protecting you from for many years," she said, "something you have never known about me. But I'm getting on now, and I think you're all old enough to hear the truth." Sons, daughters, grandchildren eyed each other nervously and steeled themselves for revelation. "All my life," the grande dame announced, "I have suffered from fallen arches."

My own parents can produce instant anxiety by the loaded "What's new?" question that begins our weekly long-distance phone call. The question sounds innocuous enough, but it really means "where will your next four by-lines appear?" And as with Chinese food, they are hungry again in half an hour. From the time I began this laggard career, my father has been enshrining its output in an excess of gilt and fine leather that the Vatican Library is mad to lay hands on. These scrapbooks are the focus of his retirement years, while my mother, for her part, name-drops periodicals. "When will that story you were writing for *The New York Times Magazine* come out?" she says. "Well, the editors have to make a decision about buying it first," I say, explaining that assignment doesn't guarantee sale. "What?" she recoils. "But I've already told my dentist!" How can I fail my gentle white-haired father by giving him nothing new to display to the breathless garbagemen he halts on their rounds each week for a glimpse at the scrapbook? How can I leave my mother with nothing to show the dentist but pyorrhea?

They were, of course, pleased for a time when a story about me appeared in the "Our Children" column of their retirement community's own newspaper. The article began straightforwardly enough, something like: "Judith Wax, daughter of Mr. and Mrs. Milton Weiss, 2014 Serenity Terrace, is a Genius." Readers who pressed on for up-to-the-minute news were rewarded by the disclosure of my 1946 election to Quakertown Junior-Senior High School National Honor Society. ("I don't know where the paper got *that*," said my pop, looking shifty.)

Who would guess that little story would cause disquietude and thunderclouds to darken those halcyon patios? I wasn't sure why, but it was clearly my fault. A woman who lived several blocks from my parents declared herself spokesperson for certain unspecified residents. Why, she wanted to know, had their children been slighted in favor of my slender accomplishments, and—most particularly—why had her son Stewart's achievements gone unheralded? ("What do you mean, what did Stewart do?" she exploded. "His wife's brother was a guest on 'Phil Donahue'!") Well, there was a lot of side taking and rancorous exchange just short of hand-to-hand combat. And though it's not as bad as my responsibility for a land war in Asia, it tweaks an over-developed midlife conscience all the same.

As for the owner of that other spectacular guilt complex, my friend Shirley, she's even further down on her luck than during the period she lashed herself to her dying mother's bedside, waiting for a loving message. Her husband has run off, leaving a string of debts for which she cosigned; the novel that was going to make her rich has been turned down by the eleventh publisher. But by some miracle, or perhaps because of Shirley's skill as bedpan wielder, her mother made a sci-ence-defying recovery, bought a wig called the Dolly Parton, and married her fifth millionaire. It's said the old lady's wed-ding was lavish, a Faroukian extravagance one guest classified as A.F.C.E.F.T.Y. (a family could eat for ten years).

I only heard about it thirdhand, though, because Shirley wasn't there. She was having a hysterectomy the week of the wedding. Her timing annoyed her mother so much, she didn't even drop in to say good-bye to her daughter in the hospital before she pinned on the Dolly Parton and flew off to honey-moon in Monaco. "I'd like your true opinion as a friend," said Shirley from her bed of pain. "How do you think I failed her?"

They Call It Doing
Your Griefwork

There's another variety of guilt that sometimes checks in with middle age. I don't know any funny stories about this kind, though, because it's so tangled up with pain, hard-nosed reality, and—most of all—friendship.

The best thing about the midyears, at least about mine, is the depth of the friendships. The worst thing can be losing them. It's to be expected that in middle age, mortality is not only intimated, but sometimes delivered, that pain and loss are birthday presents nobody asks for. Even children learn life isn't fair; a teenage girl I know wrote a poem with a line in it I wish were mine: "The dreaded are punctual." But things have gotten out of hand, the timing's way off, and the present generation of the middle-aged is suffering from an unprecedented epidemic of horror. Cancer has never before assaulted so massively and mercilessly and untimely—much of it the legacy of post–World War II technology. We got better living through chemistry, all right, and the bill is just coming due (with God knows what future cost and mutagenic dividends for our children and grandchildren). Not one of my mother's friends had cancer of the breast; only one died in middle age. I have almost as many friends *with* cancer—or steeling themselves against a second bout—as I do without. And while it's true that a few varieties of cancer are on the decline and that medical advances keep people alive longer today, longevity often means living dependent on chemicals that ravage while they rescue and in fear of new invasions yet to mobilize.

The December day the wittiest friend I've ever had came home from the hospital, I brought her homemade soup and instant lies. Both offerings were meant to comfort (me as well as her); neither could be swallowed with ease anymore. I found her at her living-room window, watching the melting snow. "I'm sitting here in a blaze of optimism," she said, "planning my garden." We both laughed, an astonished burst, then stared at each other in shocked recognition of what had been unspeakable between us, that maybe she wouldn't live to see that garden's blossoming. She didn't.

A few weeks after her funeral, the most alive, exuberant man I've ever known died, a brilliant architect, glad-hander, party cavorter, and all-around rejoicer. He was short, square-bodied as a wrestler. Two drinks and he'd lift me up and carry me around a dance floor; one more and he'd be just as likely to hoist Shel. (But then, he was a man who thought big. The last project he worked on—though he didn't live to see its topping off—was the world's tallest building.) A color photograph hangs in our study. It shows him leaping through the air in Chicago's Lincoln Park, a madly grinning urban Nijinsky; only this one is dressed in long winter underwear. His wife's handwriting over the picture gives a time and date and invites

"Come help Peter Pan celebrate his fiftieth birthday." It turned out to be Peter Pan's last frolic.

Watching people you care about get picked off is seldom a process that elevates the beholder, particularly when fear and guilt make shaming intrusions. As her disease staked new territory, I began to imagine that my friend who had planned her garden in a "blaze of optimism" had started disliking me. But it was I who disliked myself, for what seemed the vulgarity of owning a still-healthy body, for forgetting her and laughing at a party, for bursts of exaltation about my new career, and—worst of all—for the irrational fears I developed. Against all medical information, to say nothing of logic, I began to believe that I could "catch" her disease. Newspapers had been running stories about a new bit of conjecture that the herpes simplex virus responsible for cold sores might transform itself into something that produces certain forms of cancer; I'd started sprouting those crusty little herpes stigmata on my upper lip every few months and couldn't stop making a connection I *knew* was neurotic. Maybe it would have been better if I'd told her; we might have been able to laugh at me together. Instead, though I continued to see her every few days and kissed her each time, I was sure she sensed the fear in my touch, and I loathed myself for its presence.

I suppose it's another face of that fear, a shrinking back from our own mortality, that causes the dehumanizing treatment of terminal patients in so many hospitals. What else could explain the cruel incident during that same friend's last stay at one of them? She had a great natural dignity; a woman too ladylike to scream at her uninvited guest, the pain that had moved in full time. Her husband tried every distraction, including—on one visit—a bottle of Scotch. He hoped a bedtime glass of it might ease her into sleep, and it did. But a night nurse discovered the bottle, shook her awake, and began to rave about the peril of taking a drink when a few hours earlier she'd been given a sleeping pill. With another nurse's help, my friend was evicted from bed and forced to spend most of the night in a wheelchair. She was unable to walk by then; the cancer had metastasized to her bones. Her spleen, breast, and ovaries had been removed, her lungs nearly destroyed, and the pain of sitting—often a misery—was unbearable during the long hours of wheelchair banishment. Yet the pain that pierced her soul was the humiliation she felt when those two angels of vengeance punished her for one unsanctioned high-ball as though she were a bed-wetting child. Until she died a few weeks later, tears of rage at her helplessness that night still overcame her, though I'd never seen one drop shed in self-pity during years of escalating agony.

My friend the architect had planned to give a speech that Wednesday morning his wife found him lying on the floor by their bed. When I got to the hospital a few hours later, it was just in time to hear a pleasant-looking woman ask his wife, "Would you please sign this form releasing your husband's kidneys for transplant?" Until that moment, she'd rather hoped her *husband* would be released. Perhaps hospital protocol got a little out of sync that day because no one had made the "brain death" announcement before the "we have to get the kidneys while they're still warm" one.

I thought about those incidents, and my own fears, when I read about a researcher who was studying the effect of other people's reactions on the terminally ill. In order to get as close as possible to firsthand knowledge, he studied all the symptoms of abdominal cancer and its treatment and even had surgery to create authentic scars so that when he faked a "cancer recurrence" (as a stranger in a strange city), neither the doctor he consulted nor the hospital that admitted him suspected what he was up to. He was so convincing, in fact, that he was put on a floor perfect for his research, one on which every patient was considered hopeless, and treated accordingly—that is, alternately patronized and shunned. The trouble was that even though the man was healthy and could check out anytime, within a short while he became so emotionally isolated by his treatment as a nonperson that he began to *feel* ill and took on all the psychic side effects of the genuinely dying.

If we were inheritors of an Eastern culture, we might be able to take the cosmic view of small private tragedies, make long-range spiritual sense of disaster's indifference. But as the people you love are afflicted younger and younger—many of them before their parents—serene acceptance is hard to come by. It's more in the Western style to demand an accounting, deposit the accusations in the proper complaint department. That's why one of the worst shocks of middle age is finding out no one is really in charge.

Still, there are guidelines for handling the unthinkable, and in the common fear of losing control, it's comforting (at least distracting) to think that there are rules for getting a purchase on catastrophe. We've learned, for instance, about the healing powers in "doing your griefwork." We know that the brave front and stiff upper lip only defer what has to be released to be exorcised; true friends help each other to mourn it out. (Enlightenment and preparation can go too far, though. When a little girl I know arrived for a week's visit with her adoring grandparents, she brought her "favorite book" along for them to read to her at bedtime. It was titled *What to Do When Grandpa Dies.)*

A woman I've kept up with since our high school days was widowed at forty-five. She'd had what looked like a four-star marriage, the kind that makes other people secretly compare their own unions to it (and then give themselves bad reviews), so when her husband died suddenly, nobody thought she'd ever get over it. After all, they'd been in love since they were seventeen. It was, indeed, harrowing for her, but she did all that therapeutic "griefwork" right on schedule, just the way the experts recommend. Everyone around her played his or her supportive part, too; you could have filmed the whole thing for a documentary on how to do an awful thing right, and in time she seemed to have passed through all the stages of recovery. Eventually, she even fell in love again, with a man as bright, attractive, and affectionate as she is, and their marriage seemed imminent. But on the brink of eternal vows, she called it off, during what was planned as a romantic "engagement" weekend at a resort hotel. "I took one look at him—his skin was very white—floating on his back in the pool," she said, "and I knew I'd never remarry." Maybe her "never" will soften in time. At any rate, the déjà vu horror of seeing another man she loved stretched out and face up, convinced her that there was some griefwork still left for her.

Perhaps many women of my age put a particular value on friendship among our sex, and feel such despair at the losses, because we found the nourishment of that kind of closeness relatively late in life. Despite the "best friend" rituals of girlhood, most of us grew up wary of our gender. My mother's caution to me—"You can't really trust another girl"—was a fairly standard one. Some of us are only beginning to sheathe the rivalrous edge that cuts you off from real intimacy; who knows whether the breakthroughs owe more to feminist influences or to the natural affinity of those who shared the excesses of a couple of crazy decades?

Joint bewilderment is a powerful bond. If two women have supported each other through the worst trials of contemporary parenting, and perhaps wept alternately and unabashedly into each other's everyday-ware coffee cups, they're not likely to worry about which of them gets to play femme fatale at a Saturday night neighborhood gathering (whatever their girlhood conditioning). Which is not to claim that true supportiveness is a 100 percent fail-safe, twenty-four-hour girdle. "I love my neighbor dearly," a woman told me, "but I've always been jealous of her gorgeous skin. When her husband died suddenly, she really fell to pieces and I felt so sorry for her that I often sat up nights with her and cooked and did everything I could to help her through it. But there was this damn little teenaged bitch's voice in my head that kept whispering, 'So if she's really that upset, *how come she doesn't get wrinkles?*' "

When a woman is widowed in middle age—a time in life we like to think of as too young for the job—the event can set off the same fears, denials, and dread of "catching it" among her contemporaries that illness sometimes does. And it can be as isolating and devastating as if she *were* diseased. A woman who has had chilling, firsthand experience of such freeze-out told me she suffers from "widow's quarantine." "It's interesting to guess about the psychological reasons some of your friends drop you," she said, "except it usually hurts too much to be clinical about. When Jack was alive, we were invited out so often that I imagined all those people thought I was special; now I know I was only *half* special. I guess it's childish of me, but when somebody whose life is pretty much intact comes on smug to me, I really have to fight the temptation to growl at her, '*Watch* it, lady!' "

Like the woman who offended her neighbor by mourning too attractively, middle-aged widows sometimes find themselves victims of the kinds of rivalrous feelings that haven't been out in full force since the month before their junior proms. "What's worse than *that*," said a woman who'd been widowed for two years at forty-nine, "is to know you're *not* a threat to anybody's marriage. I'd feel a lot better if I could comfort myself that I'm left out so much because I'm considered a danger to husbands, rather than knowing that it's really because I make the uneven number that louses up seating arrangements or I'm 'tōō old' to be invited as a dinner partner for an unattached man my own age. Most of the women I know are a lot more threatened by divorcées than widows anyhow; there seems to be a prevailing philosophy that the widow gets a pat on the head and the divorcée gets hers on the fanny. It's very degrading, of course, to be the victim of that kind of uninvited pawing, but once in a while I sort of wish somebody would give me the chance to make a speech of indignation!" (A friend of hers, also widowed, has advised her to flee the suburbs for an apartment in Chicago, as she herself has done. "It was like the ark out there," the refugee said with a little shudder. "I figured it was take to the bottle or the city.")

In a just world, if you had to be allotted widowhood, you'd get a chance to do it like Madame Max, in the TV version of Trollope's Palliser stories. That's what *I'd* choose, anyway; the lady was gorgeous, rich, charming, witty, madly adored, and all of it while wearing becoming hats. But in hard everyday existence, the widows I happen to know who are going it alone best are the ones absorbed by brain and hand in something to which they are committed—a job, a cause, a craft. "Maybe I've made my work come first in my life now," said a widow in her fifties, "because it's something I can give myself to and at the same time exert a lot of control over. It also gives me an entrée into the social world that isn't based on pity or duty, it gives me something new to talk about, and the best part is that I don't have to wait for it to telephone." Not that the rewarding career is hanging around out there, just waiting to spark someone's life. After six months of pavement pounding and dead-end leads, a widowed friend said wearily, "I've been offered two affairs, one hand in marriage, and no jobs."

One friend who got the job she dreamed about was luckier, except she had guilt attacks (no one's safe) to go with it. "I know that if Leonard hadn't died, I'd never have begun working," she said. "And now I like my job so much—and forget him so often—that I'm sometimes overwhelmed by feelings of callousness and disloyalty."

Another woman I know had told me, "When I'm feeling alone and rotten, I force myself to acknowledge that if he'd lived, we'd probably be divorced by this time." But, unlike her, my friend with the guilt seizures said, "The most peculiar part of it is that I had what I considered to be a happy marriage; I was contented. That's why I'm so ashamed to find myself blaming him sometimes because I didn't start to work years ago. What was he supposed to do, order me out of the house? Or maybe die even younger for the good of my career?"

"I've always worked," said a fifty-one-year-old woman. "I love what I do, and it gets me through a great deal. But for me, widowhood is one big grayness. What I miss in my life is enthusiasm. Even with the job, time hangs heavy. When Ken died, every widow in town called and said 'Now we can be friends!' I had to bite my tongue to keep from saying, 'But *why?*' I sometimes see other widows shopping aimlessly, keeping up halfhearted gaieties at lunches with each other. I have to keep telling myself like a litany, 'I'm one of you now.' Who wants to celebrate a triumph alone? Who wants to travel alone?"

"That part about travel is only logistics panic," said another woman I talked to. "I used to suffer from it, too, until I forced myself to put my act together, and I'm very exhilarated by the feeling that I'm grown-up enough to do the things that were always done for me. I know I'm damn lucky to have been left without the financial worry most women my age have, and that what I've done is only a small advance. But I can't help being just a little pleased with myself that I can find a bathroom anywhere in the world!"

It must be true that trouble comes not singly, because both those women were dealt midlife disaster in matched pairs, cancer to complement their bereavement. "After a mastectomy, hysterectomy, chemotherapy, and two horrible years of sweating it out," one of them told me, "I recently went through all the tests again and got the report that I'm in a state of complete remission. I walked home on air from the hospital, thinking fantastic, fan*tas*tic. It didn't hit me until later how Ken and I would have celebrated the news. Now, of course, I have another problem—I have to face life. All this time, I've been in emotional limbo, behaving well, going about my duties, but never thinking about the future, or relationships, or about *myself*. All I focused on was the disease, as though it were a separate entity, and missing Ken. He's receding now; I'm sorry about that, because it's almost like we're losing touch when a day passes and he hasn't been on my mind very much. I feel sad, but not depressed; I guess it's all a necessary part of letting go. And now that I'm reasonably sure I'm going to live, I have to come to grips with the quality of that living, not just the fact of it."

I asked her if quality meant another man to change the "one big grayness" she'd described as her current view of life into something in a more vibrant color. "I'm not sure I'll ever be able to show my body to a man again," she said, a big woman with the earthy kind of Colleen Dewhurst beauty that made our generation of mothers-in-law advise those who had it to "get a nice permanent, dear." "Not that I was ever Miss World, but my body was whole, I liked it, and it served me. I guess I'm even more afraid of pity than rejection. Pity infuriates me; I feel diminished by it. Maybe I can only get the sensitivity I'm looking for from another woman, but I've been a lifelong happy heterosexual, and if surgery changed the way my body happens to look, it didn't change what it wants. Or what it remembers, either."

When I was in sixth grade, "imitating Miss Redlinger" was a favorite party trick. It didn't require much skill to mimic her shrieking outbursts or the way she would glower at us like a furious owl and bite on the tip of her tongue. I was ashamed to tell my friends that although she made me and the class bad boy move our desks smack up against hers ("Judith is the worst chatterbox in Pennsylvania"), I liked her better than all her gentle predecessors. At least I liked school best that year, because Miss Redlinger let us read a lot of fiction and write our own stories, and mine made her laugh out loud—as riveting an outburst as her screams.

But Miss Redlinger's tirades, though we mocked them at parties, scared us into respectful silence, particularly when she'd chase some knickered boy around the classroom at the point of her umbrella. That's when she'd yell her famous "I'm after your *blood!*" and we were pretty sure she really was. As long as it wasn't my own, I sort of hoped to see a drop or two.

It didn't occur to me for years that our teacher may at times have been crazed with pain or her own terrors. She would cradle her immensely distorted, mottled right arm against her body like a nightmare sausage, and a boy I hated (he would flick a mirror under your dress when you walked to the pencil sharpener) said her arm was swollen like that because "Old lady Redlinger had her tits cut off." Our parents were more decorous, but vague. "She isn't well," they said. Only a few of them could manage the word *cancer,* and none that even more indelicate one *breasts.*

My fear started in sixth grade and never left me: I suspect the other eleven-year-old girls in her class have carried Miss Redlinger with them into middle age, too. But fear would have come to us anyway; to be female is to inherit that legacy of dread—wherever you grew up, whether you actually saw the effects of a maiming or only felt them in the place breasts of your own hadn't even shown up yet.

Women today who have had mastectomies don't seem to look like Miss Redlinger; my own friends—in public, at least—are unmarked. And because of the candor and courage of Betty Ford and Happy Rockefeller, we have been shown living proof that femininity goes deeper than the knife. Those two women probably saved lives (though there is the usual confusion over whether detection procedures will take others) and doubtless gave heart to women throughout the country. They were selfless, maybe even heroic. I couldn't help wondering, though, if there were some who compared their own experiences and felt isolated or somehow inferior—women with less supportive partners, or none at all, with no one to admire their courage or notice its lack, without money or strength for fashion's pretty palliatives. Most people struggle against the unthinkable with the best they can muster; some of us have top-of-the-line, high-quality machinery for coping, others have to put lesser equipment in gear (and even the best can wear out).

A man I know, a crossed-finger survivor of prostate cancer surgery and therapy, said, "What has to be invented for people with their backs against the wall is some alternative to the middle of the night." My widowed friend whose cancer is in remission agreed. "But I've always been willing to meet the morning, no matter what horrors the night brought," she said. "There's glory in my shower, my cup of coffee, the structure in my job, a child's voice outside my window. And I'm never late, not ever, not for anything!"

Long ago Shel and I "belonged" to something called the Lagoon Club, ten or fifteen families who would gather at the Lincoln Park lagoon on Sunday afternoons in summer. Our kids would play and squabble; we'd picnic and grill hot dogs on a portable barbecue, city people playing Extended Family *sur l'Herbe*. We don't gather anymore; we're too picked over. Only two of those families have made it intact until now (at least they seem intact by whatever criteria for wholeness you can apply without crawling into other people's lives and beds). As for the rest of us, divorce, death, disease, and/or kid catastrophe claimed our membership and attention over the intervening years, and though it hasn't *all* been soaper-style Sturm und Drang, I look back on those casual Sunday barbecues as the days of our innocence. Some of us might have chewed our potato chips with less complacency if we'd known that what was ahead was hardly a picnic. I suppose the handbook for midlife might be called *I Never Promised You a Lagoon Club*; like most people, we expected more considerate trauma or a chance to pick and choose something palatable from the groaning board of griefs—and to do it later, of course, always later. (When my dearest old friend Carole and I were young mothers, we took a sacred vow that the first of us to succumb to dimming eyesight could *depend* on the other to shave her legs for her as long as we both should live. Having disposed in advance of the worst that far-off middle age might hurl at us, we settled ourselves into deck chairs in our tract-home driveways and spoke of other weighty matters while our children spooned dirt into each other's mouths.)

There are happy stories, of course; solid recoveries from the rim of disaster, better-than-ever good health, untouched families, unscathed lives. That was the way it always looked for Shel's old fraternity brother (let's call him Preston Perlvogle), a fifty-year-old who unfailingly came back from his annual physical examination to report that he had the "heart and prostate of a teenager." So we were alarmed to learn when we had dinner with Preston and his wife one night that he'd been barely able to haul himself around since a bizarre symptom had begun afflicting him. "I don't want to upset or embarrass you," he said with a nod toward me, "but I've got this terrible rash on my behind, these bright red *perfect little circles* that almost look like someone drew them with a compass. And just when I breathe easy that they've gone away, the damn things pop out again, brighter than the time before."

"What does your doctor say?" both of us asked.

"He can't say anything," Preston moaned, "because I make an appointment to see him, and then the plague disappears before I can even get my pants down. I'm thinking of moving into his house, so the next time I get an attack, I can moon on the spot."

"Preston's not telling you the whole thing," his wife said tearfully. "What really scares him is that he served in the tropics in forty-five, you know, and he says he's heard about cases where those awful parasite infections were dormant for years and years and then wrecked people for the rest of their lives!" Preston began to sweat as though we were dining in Guadalcanal.

After more weeks of dermal anxiety, Preston changed doctors; he even found a guy who'd trained in tropical diseases. The man turned out to be a superb diagnostician. Without one lab test or X-ray, without any letting of blood or urine, without so much as a glimpse at those beleaguered buttocks, he asked the exact two questions that cured Preston of his life-threatening "perfect little circles," probably forever.

"Mr. Perlvogle," he said, "do you take many baths?"

"Oh," said Preston, "I do, I do!"

"Mr. Perlvogle," said the doctor, "how long ago did you put a new rubber mat in your bathtub?"

When Preston's friends heard the story, they were reduced to tears that, for once, had nothing to do with mourning. It made a nice change.

World of Our Mothers

My mother has her own philosophy about grief. She thinks that a great deal of it could be avoided if people only paid enough attention to proper posture. Despite those mill ends masquerading as the real goods that life has occasionally palmed off on her, I know she believes that misfortune is slower to slip it to persons who "look nice" (and she certainly always did).

That sappy old saying "If you want to know what your bride is going to look like in twenty years, take a good look at her mother" used to cheer me a lot. I hoped, when I was young, any potential admirer of mine would do just that; my mother was a dish. But it's highly unlikely that any suitor, anywhere, ever married or dumped his beloved because of previews of coming attractions (or atrocities). It's women themselves who cast a cold eye on their progenitors. And in our middle years, the appraisal often takes on a new earnestness, though not just to see how we'll look. "Will I act, feel, live like she does?" we ask ourselves—some of us in admiration, many in nail-chewing terror. (Shirley, in her obsessive solicitude for that self-worshiping mother of hers, may simply be trying to prove the difference between them.)

We search for clues in mental film clips of the past and family albums. "My God, I'm three years older than Mother was in these pictures from my wedding!" "When Mother was the age I am now, I'd made her a grandmother twice." It starts us speculating about them as other women, like—and unlike—ourselves. What were their secrets when those photographs were taken? Have we ever really known these people? Did they know themselves?

Small, graceful, looking (in her boyish bob) like a young Julie Harris, my mother laughs out of an old snapshot and startles me with her beauty. Or maybe it's the uninhibited, head-thrown-back laughter that startles; she looks withdrawn and troubled, if not angry, in other fading photographs. Though my father and I dreaded explosions of that anger, we were grateful and dazzled that "Lili the beauty" belonged to us. In some of the snapshots, my mother hugs me, a Depression tot dressed up in hats-to-match and white-gloved finery my parents couldn't afford (at three I had a derby and leather coat). But in later pictures, Lili stares at her only child, the scrawny Girl Scout with long blond braids, as if to say, "Who are you? What are you expecting?"

My mother carries around her own headful of old scenes. The most important one begins without a sound track; she is five years old and wakes in the big house outside Budapest to a silence she will always hear. Little Lili wasn't told she was going to be left behind with the servants and her tyrannical German grandparents when her mother, father, and sister Olga sailed to America in 1914. "We didn't want to upset her,"

Nana, my grandmother, once explained to me tearfully. "We were only intending to visit the American cousins." But the war began, and if my grandfather had gone back to Hungary, he would have been forced to serve with his regiment of Hussars, an assignment (according to my mother) for which he had little taste. That aversion served him well; his entire regiment was wiped out in Russia.

Lili didn't hear from her parents again for five years. They wrote her many times, my grandmother said, and sent packages, but nothing ever got through until the telegram all those years later announcing that a sister, Ruth, had been born in America. "She thinks we abandoned her," my grandmother told me. "My God, she'll never forgive us, not till everybody's dead." (No, Nana, she couldn't and not after, either.)

My mother was nearly twelve when she came to this country and was met at the station in Pennsylvania by my grandparents and Milton, the seventeen-year-old American cousin who came to meet her in his new yellow roadster. *"Ist das der Herr Chauffeur?"* said my mother, pointing imperiously to the cousin. He was, instead, her future Herr Husband, my father-to-be.

My mother stares ahead coldly and describes herself, the five-year-old racing through the big house in Hungary, looking wildly under all the beds to see if her older sister, Olga, was hiding beneath one of them (even the bed that had belonged to their little sister, Magda, until she died in the influenza epidemic a few months before). "All that was under Olga's bed was a pleated skirt," says my mother. "I can't look at a pleated skirt even today without feeling the panic return." She started screaming for her sister Olga, then for her parents "when I saw that Mama's best dresses were gone from the closets."

On days my mother was judged "bad" by the servants

over the next seven years, her own clothes were locked away in one of those closets as punishment. I wonder how often the beautiful little Hungarian girl thought that her "badness" had made her parents leave her. And years later, when the anger that sent her shrieking and flailing at us tore through her (and so shamed her that once she made me cut an account of it out of my eighth-grade diary), I wonder how often she thought my father and I would show *our* true colors someday and desert her, too.

The years I was growing up in Quakertown, that little Pennsylvania Dutch town where my father also had been born, Lili spent at least half of every day shut in her room. She was reading: the lives of England's monarchs, Ford Madox Ford, Malraux, the Russians. She'd once begged to go to college, but her father explained that there wasn't enough money, and besides, why would a girl (and such a pretty one) need an education? So she married Milton, the American second cousin. Not long ago I was looking at one of her old volumes of Yeats's work and found she'd tucked the poet's obituary away in it in 1939, as proprietary a gesture as if she were Maud Gonne. But then my mother permitted Yeats access to feelings she didn't allow the perfidious living.

She sometimes writes wonderful letters to me—dangerously witty, proudly erudite—but she doesn't know how to write a check, dispatch a bill, or drive a car. Nor does she usually venture as far as the shopping center near their retirement village without my father, who spoils her past redemption, going along for what she calls "moral support." Once her sister Ruth said, "For heaven's sake, Lili, can't you put your own wristwatch on and off without Milton's help?" "What?" said my mother, all indignation. "Do you expect me to do it with *one hand?*"

Not long ago, she suddenly looked at me and said, "The

day before I got married, a beau of mine I was quite fond of appeared and begged me to marry him instead of your father." I visualized Dustin Hoffman in a twenties version of *The Graduate,* kidnapping his gorgeous beloved from the very brink of "I do."

"You never told me that, Mother," I said. "Who was he?"

She stared at me for a minute with the big hazel eyes my father has forbidden her to leave to science (because he can't bear to think of her altered), then summoned that ever-faithful one. "Milton," she commanded, "what *was* my boyfriend's name?"

Sometimes I suspect it took me so long to start writing because she wanted me—as I probably wanted my own children—to do it *instead* of her. Maybe I started at last because I was afraid that my life (half of it spent, like hers, reading in a bedroom) was turning into another too scantily used.

For most of us, though, it isn't fear of becoming our mother that sends us back to our memories and the mirror watching for her. If, as we ourselves age, we look in fear, it's of impending membership in America's least popular, most discriminated-against club . . . the society of "old women." And compared to the isolation, unsexing, and depersonalizing processes with which this country freezes out its aging women, the old Eskimo custom of depositing granny on an ice floe was warmhearted. (At least she understood her contribution to a sort of Arctic Malthusianism.) In *our* culture, older women get put on ice psychically. Which is why, as we tiptoe or crash into middle age, some of us see each alteration of face and body as an announcement that The Ice Floe Cometh. I saw my own future in the Weber *New Yorker* cartoon of the "with it" dowager (a geriatric Gidget in fun fur jacket, flared pants, bizarrely voguish makeup) who is telling her elderly peer at the bus stop, "I used to be old, too, but it wasn't my cup of tea."

For many people, fear of forgetfulness outranks all other age dreads. A few women I know began doing crossword puzzles in midlife as a kind of brain exercise, their rationale: "I work out my body lumps on a mat at the gym, but I haven't forced my head into regular workouts since I quit my job twenty-five years ago, before my first child was born." Part of the fear is based on what we *expect* may happen, what we've observed among people we've known, the feeling of incompetence the first time we can't remember a good friend's name during an introduction. But no one knows yet why we age at different rates and why certain cells call it quits when they do, why my friend Harriet, at eighty-five, has Chicago's most gorgeous brain (it's worth noting she has flexed it daily all her life and probably started out with trillions more cells than most people) or why two other very bright women I've known had such severe cases of premature hardening of the brain's arteries that they were virtually senile by their late fifties.

After Paul's bad time and hospitalization, I began having trouble remembering things I *knew* that I knew. Names, book titles, word meanings, what I was about to say, or had just read, fluttered from my head and left me running through the alphabet for clues. I was forty-two then, and in a kind of terror that I was becoming like those two prematurely senile women I'd known and admired, I went to a neurologist and sputtered out my anxiety. "It's amazing," said this eminent healer, "how some people will talk themselves into aging."

"But I *hate* forgetting things," I almost pleaded. "It really scares me." And I told him what I knew about those two women who haunted me, that both were not only very intelligent, but stable, apparently happy and hardly self-punishers.

"I'm not impressed by the evidence," he said, indulgently patting the head that worried me. "As I told you, people talk themselves into aging." He's so distinguished and respected that, frankly, I backed out of his office feeling pretty foolish. But I wish I'd thought to ask him one more question: "Tell me, Dr. G., why did you decide to lose your hair?"

Two weeks after she'd had a stroke, I came upon Julia, a zippy octogenarian I dearly love, crying in her hospital bed. She wept in shame, she told me, because a foot-tapping intern had just demanded, "Who's the vice-president?" and she couldn't get a fix on Walter Mondale. (In the regrettable days when the correct answer would have been Spiro Agnew, Julia's temporary block could have been the healthiest response, and though that intern's question might be a standard one for checking orientation, it's far from conclusive.)

Julia was already suffering what most of us dread—loss of control, loss of the person we used to be. Luckily, her middle-aged daughter understands that self-esteem has the same right to recovery as the body, and she taught her refined mother to meet that intern's next challenge, should it come, with an ever-so-sweet-voiced "Screw off, sonny!" A few days later, Julia was collected enough to tell him not only that, but explain a few ramifications the young doctor neither asked for nor had known about Carter's latest energy proposal.

Partly as research, partly in fear, I tried to find out a bit more about memory loss and brain changes by attending a meeting devoted to that subject. The conferees were a group of psychiatrists, psychologists, social workers, and laymen who gather monthly to discuss new approaches to the problems of aging. They call themselves the Society for Life Cycle Psychology and Aging, and what impressed me when I sat in on sessions of this Chicago-based group is their acknowledgment of what *isn't* known.

At the meeting concerned with memory problems, there was fascinating import in one specialist's presentation of his findings among older female patients whose primary complaint was forgetfulness. Most of their husbands complained about these women's forgetfulness, too, but tests showed that it was *they* who usually had more acute memory problems than their wives. The couples tested seemed to have worked out—however unconsciously—a conspiracy of roles; they'd tacitly agreed that *she* would play the one with failing memory. Most of the "forgetful" wives did better on the memory tests not only than their husbands, but also than their peers in general. Perhaps they were merely more sensitive, or more demanding of themselves, or valued brain function more. It's also possible that the report was just another bit of theorizing. But there does seem a warning in it (for us in midlife) to question some of the roles assigned to us before we dutifully act them out for the rest of our lives. And I wish that I could have found out more about memory loss and brain change at that meeting, but I disgraced myself by having to bolt from it in the middle of the session because I suddenly couldn't remember whether I'd turned my headlights off (a similar lapse that week had already cost me twenty-two dollars in towing charges).

Though I left before summing-up time, it's doubtful anyone could have made a more pungent evaluation than my pal Bessie when we talked about the general problem. Bessie lives communally with eleven other elderly widows and says she often wishes that her eighty-eight-year-old brain were not in its impeccable shape because it makes her too acutely aware of *other* losses. "It isn't the vacancy in the head that hurts most, darling," said Bessie, "it's the one in the heart."

Sometimes it's more unsettling to think we may become one of the total recallers, rather than one of the "forgetters." You can, of course, be both, since recent memory is the first to "go," while that part of the brain that cooks old chestnuts frequently boils on as long as life does. (You see the problem coming, as I do, when you can't remember who was at that dinner for eight last week, but have preserved intact all celebrants' names at your fourth birthday party.) When older people reminisce minutely, they are making us gifts of themselves, appointing us curators of their histories. And most of us who squirm as soon as an elderly acquaintance trots out a new round of Remembrances of Things Past haven't gotten around to discovering what we miss by automatic tune-out.

It would be condescending to suggest that a well-seasoned bore is any more palatable than a youthful one. But I've been around the country talking to teens, college students, and women of my age, as well as the elderly, and for wit, daring, originality, poignancy, and poetry, nobody outclasses that maligned person we're afraid to be cornered into becoming someday—"the old woman." No other generation has nearly as many straight talkers, truth stalkers, joke lovers. Despite our decade-long ululations in praise of *Openness!,* no other group I've interviewed comes close to elderly women in risking revelation of authentic feelings. (When we aren't shutting them up and out, of course.) And one of the compensations of middle age is to discover that you are learning occasionally to tell that inexorable self-censor (just as Julia learned to tell the officious intern), "Screw off, sonny!"

Whatever happens to our lives and bodies, the voice in our heads doesn't age much. Sure, we struggle for "maturity," but the voice goes on talking to us with the same urgency it did on our first day in kindergarten, the day our first child went to school, as it will (or already has) the day our first grandchild becomes a pencil box carrier. I like the way an elderly gentleman expressed it to a young woman who stopped to help him with some heavy parcels. They lingered at his door, chatting for a while, and—no longer quite strangers—agreed that it would be nice to talk again. As she turned and began to walk away, she heard him call after her, "Young lady! I dream the same dreams *you* do!"

Not that romanticizing the elderly, or our own futures in the ranks of them, is an improvement over indifference. In age, most of us will become ripened versions of our standard selves, exaggerations, perhaps, of what we are now. Shirley's narcissistic mother, for instance, simply fell deeper in love with herself. Well, we can't all be salty, wise, or—God forbid—sweet old things. I know an Attila-tempered, brilliant woman of seventy-three who has made me pledge on my life that if certain signs she considers giveaways to impending incompetence appear, I'll be the first to let her know. "You must swear to call it to my attention," she said, "if you notice that I'm acting benevolent and cheerful a lot or if I start saying things like 'Aren't people wonderful!' I simply couldn't bear to go on living that way!"

Another cherished pal, who's eighty-five, has extracted a different vow. "If I get to the stage where I start repeating my stories," she said, *"those who care for me* will kindly just say so." We have, indeed, shared some moments of truth, but it has fallen to *her* to say (very gently), "Judy, my dear, you told me that story last week."

Because I admire both these women so much, I look to them for hints on how to age well, on why some women maintain the kind of self-esteem and sociability that makes people of all ages want to be around them. The lady who dreads lapsing into cheerfulness has taken on several new projects this year: a class in poetry writing and one in home repairs. The other woman watches the state of the arts, China, Washington, scientific theory ("I heard two men who were sitting behind me at a concert discussing black holes in space, so I consulted them about where to get more information, and now I'm subscribing to a fascinating new journal"), and the foibles of our times. She serves, and actively, on the boards of many organizations, sets her alarm clock to ring so that, if absorbed in a phone conversation, she won't talk past Cronkite time, and once became so enchanted with pimp couture ("Don't you *love* those sensuous colors?") that she staked out a rather risky pimp-watching post from which to continue her scholarly observations. The world returns her passionate interest in it; I know a dozen people half her age who claim her as "best friend."

Both these women have suffered assault—the illnesses and death of children and husbands—and both have painful physical problems. One is well-off, the other nearly penniless, but they share continuing engagement; what their newspapers tell them each day is infinitely more interesting to them than what their mirrors do (though both are strikingly, and painstakingly, attractive). And whatever sneak attacks fate has prepared for them, they have stayed participants in a larger sphere than self-concern. Of course, there is luck involved: happy combinations of genes and temperament, clear heads, bodies that have rebelled, but not quit. You can't place an advance order for those little items, yet if there is any hint to us in middle age from such women, it is to leap into the world *now*—while our legs have some spring to them—so involvement outside the narrowness of self becomes a habit that keeps us willing parts of life.

And what of the life of the body? In a society dedicated to the proposition that only firm breasts merit firm erections, there has been no more rigidly observed denial imposed on aging people (especially women) than the taboos against their sexuality. The denial process began for most of us in childhood, when it was unthinkable that your very own parents were "doing it." The trouble is that we go on withholding permission, and as people age, many withhold it from themselves. When we get the idea that need isn't "nice," body will listen to psyche; the most sensitive sexual organ has always been the brain. Doctors often convey their own childhood-rooted disapproval, if not amusement or repugnance, when aging patients work up the nerve to discuss their sexual concerns. I know an analyst who had to go back into treatment when he learned that his eighty-year-old recently remarried father had inquired of the family physician, "I've slowed down a little, doc; do you think three times a week is enough to keep the bride and me healthy?"

A meeting of gerontologists concluded, auspiciously for us, that our mothers' generation is likely to be the last in America to be forced into automatic neutering. More accepting attitudes toward aging and sexuality—and our own evidence in midlife that sexual feelings continue, may grow, and even explode—augurs well. But with over-sixty-five widows currently outnumbering their male counterparts five to three, expressing those feelings may be as difficult for us, someday, as it is for today's older unattached woman. And there are other unknown factors yet to be investigated. Though Duke University studies indicate that sex can be a continuing activity for people even into their nineties, as one elderly skeptic (whose research has been confined to the retirement hotel where she lives) observed, "Who can tell how long a woman *can* if a man *can't?*" Her over-eighty friend down the hall, a tiny wisp of a white-haired lady in elastic stockings, said that even if she *did* find a partner "in this desert of widows," she had no intention of remarrying. "Not," she said, "until I find out if the fellow can still get it up!"

Such technicalities aside, though, it's nice to expect that we may be allowed an openness about our needs we couldn't allow our own elders. Though most of us are no more eager for detailed accounts of the life in our parents' beds than we are of our children's (or they for ours), it's reassuring to know the possibilities. On the other hand, to be forced into geriatric sexiness, past need, desire, or ability, could be as devastating as the old neutering tradition. Physical problems, certain medications, general slowing down can inhibit or end sexual performance, and libido comes in as many variations as people do. You can almost foresee the same sort of pressures put on an aging woman as her granddaughter may have had to cope with if she happened to be that pariah among her peers, a teenaged virgin.

Like some of those middle-aged wives I interviewed who were having first affairs, many older women I talked to referred to late sexual discoveries. Others said they suspected they'd "missed out on it all." Of the "discoverers," a growing number were senior live-togethers—widows (and an occasional never-married) who shared rooms, but not marriage licenses, with aging beloveds. And though attitudes of a pre-liberation lifetime didn't always permit them to level even with themselves about such unions, they ranged from those who said there was sustenance enough in "just holding each other" to those who reported "we try all positions; Alex Comfort hasn't heard of everything."

This seventies phenomenon of late-life cohabiting is probably less a development of Hugh Hefner's department than of Health, Education, and Welfare's. Since widows who rewed must usually forfeit part of their Social Security income (though a change in the law is imminent), older couples have found that by pooling their benefits, they can wind up with slightly more than if they had married. The saving may not be much, but soaring dog food sales, according to supermarket managers, tell more about grandpa's diet than Fido's. For some elderly couples, living together has meant the difference between dining on macaroni casserole and Ken-L Ration *à deux.*

It is a commonplace dilemma of middle age that just as our children grow up and leave us with some unaccustomed breathing space, our parents often show the first signs of dependency. Many older people, of course, are able to manage autonomously, healthily, happily; others begin making increasing demands—if only unspoken ones. Whether we work out a mutually satisfying system of supports, or whether everyone gets brutalized in the process, has been a traditional problem of the middle-age rite of passage. What has been new, for *my* caught-between generation, are situations like the one my friend Jean found herself confronting recently. Several weeks after Jean's collegiate daughter and her boyfriend had been home for a midsemester visit, her elderly father arrived for a weekend with his retirement home "friend." "Is it fair," said Jean, "this should happen to a woman like me who was raised to think sex-before-marriage guaranteed instant thunderbolts and *then* had to listen to my own kids' lectures about how repressed my generation is? I ask you, is it fair that twice in one month I have had to face both my father and his roomie and my daughter and *hers* and watch them sulk when I assigned separate bedrooms? And let me tell you, *both* times I heard footsteps in the hall in the middle of the night and found myself whispering the same prayer, 'Please, Lord, I'm not a prude, just—I beg you—don't let me hear anybody's mattress!'"

Jean recently bought earplugs she hopes she'll never have to use; other middle-aged children find they can't shut out parental amour quite that easily. At one retirement hotel I often visit, an octogenarian pair named Becky and Barney were the despair of his fiftyish sons. According to the switchboard operator, the couple could be found in each other's rooms at all hours of the night; it drove the sons wild and sent them raging to the management. Sherry, the hotel's social director, loved the old pair. "You should have seen them when they were sent to this place four years ago," she told me. "Two corpses, no interest in living. Then they met each other, and they've been beaming ever since. Neither one could make it here without the other one—I think they even help each other on the potty, and I *know* they neck in the hotel theater." But despite tiny Becky's wide-eyed "Barney and me only kiss; God wouldn't want you should sleep with a fella you're not engaged," and regardless of Sherry-the-social-director's protests that they might die without each other, Becky and Barney were shipped off to separate nursing homes. Becky couldn't manage at the hotel without him, and Barney's sons insisted he had to be "saved from that woman." "Let's face it," Sherry said. "Barney's kids just don't like the girl he goes with."

Maybe what really disturbed Barney's balding "kids" most was not the possibility that their father still had a sex life, but his declarations that gentle little Becky was "the first woman I ever loved." It wasn't clear to me whether he had forgotten, blacked out, or remembered only too well his late wife. But those of us who have reached midlife without ever having experienced an all-consuming passion can take heart from the number of other "I'm in love for the first time" declarations I've heard from gray-haired sweethearts.

Still, love's maiden voyage can be bumpy at any age. Though some ladies confided, "He's made me feel like a woman for the first time!" one who had never married described agonizing seizures of "first time in my life" murderous jealousy. "I don't blame her," said the elderly object of her obsession, "the women around here just won't let me alone!" The two recently got married, but apparently there's green-eyed grief in Eden, too, since the groom complained that though she permitted him occasional solo forays to the Safeway, he was required to phone in his whereabouts every half hour. "Would you believe it?" he asked, looking pleased. "She accuses me of making dates with the checkout ladies!"

My friend Jean with her earplugs and Barney's straitlaced boys would have gotten a mouthful from Clara, a jaunty seventy-four-year-old "I'm not ready to marry" widow I met in a run-down apartment hotel. Clara called her seedy quarters "good as the Ritz," at least since she'd been sharing them—and ecstatic bubble baths—with the gentleman she loves. "I told my children, accept it or not, Jim is the big thing in my life now. Why should I sleep alone and lonely and let some other woman grab him? I know I'm getting old, and my skin could use an ironing, but Jim says my body is beautiful, and what do my children have to tell me more interesting than that?" Clara's children were accepting and pleased; so were her married grandchildren. One of them even sent her some musk-scented bubble bath for the daily double.

Not everyone, at any age, is (or wants to be) as candid as Clara. But many older women discuss their sex lives with a candor that might startle their emancipated granddaughters. A Mary Worth look-alike was all clinical poise when she explained to me how she'd taught her "inhibited" second husband (both are seventy) about oral sex. "His late wife didn't approve of it," she explained while he beamed, "but Arthur's a fast learner." Another woman had been conducting "this sort of afternoon therapy group," until a young maid at the retirement hotel where she lives caught her flagrante delicto with a matched pair of gentlemen and complained to the management that maybe those eighty-year-old hearts could take such goings-on, but *hers* couldn't. Well, she wasn't the only domestic to dampen elder ardor. I know a wealthy widow who, at sixty-nine, was thriving on her first affair until the housekeeper she'd employed for thirty years threatened to quit the recently debauched premises. "It was a terrible decision to have to make," said the widow, "but what is maturity if you haven't learned to evaluate your own priorities? So naturally I told Harold it was all over between us."

My parents, like the majority of over-sixty-five Americans, are still an autonomous, if very interdependent, couple, fortunate enough to have health, savings, options (and aware that a serious assault on the first could jeopardize the other two). They've chosen retirement village living, in a community that has chain-fenced and barbed-wired itself off from the uninvited world. The residents resent allusions to the concentration camp aspects of such rigid security methods. After all, they point out, they can even stroll out alone at night in a part of the world where daily headlines inform CRIMINALS MAKE ELDERLY PRISONERS IN THEIR OWN HOMES and YOUTH GANGS TERRORIZE OLD-TIME RESIDENTS. Most of the middle-class retirees in my parents' village praise their way of living— the ease of getting to nearby shopping and cities, the clubhouses, classes, and dances—and when I visit the pool, I do get a sense of people savoring full-time vacation, if sometimes a little defensively. (My parents report that the name of the community's man-made body of water had to be changed when too many residents protested that "Lake Serenity sounds too much like Lake Senility.")

As distraction from their neighborhood's shattering peacefulness, I take up my hobby of rummaging through family photographs when I visit my parents, and find a picture of them as honeymooners on a boat deck. My mother is sitting on her young groom's lap, wearing a cloche and flapperish chemise, her white-stockinged legs chorus girl shapely. My father, hell-bent to achieve seriousness, has grown a mustache in keeping with his new responsibilities. I want to shout at them, "Wait, wait, you're just children!" (Claudia, their youngest grandchild, is older now than they were in that snapshot.) When I was young and could sometimes hear the lap-sitting flapper's bitter tone behind closed doors, I thought I knew everything there was to know about those two people. Now I hear their voices murmuring behind other closed doors and catch a note of such seasoned complicity that it surprises me and reminds me of all I *don't* know. In my parents' world, no one "nice" got divorced; people parted by death's permission only. Which of those half century—give or take a decade— marriages are nourishing, deep, voluntary? Which are preserved in bile, resignation, or historical imperative?

I am struck and sometimes chilled by the frequency with which older women will suddenly burst out, "Enjoy your husband while you have him!" There are follow-ups to this message: "It was so sudden, and we never got a chance to travel" and "If I hadn't been dearly loved, I wouldn't find sexual repression so agonizing" and "You can't catch a worse disease than loneliness." You hear the wistful warnings from friends' mothers, department store saleswomen, pushers of stocked-for-one grocery carts. I once even got an angry "Don't think your life will *always* be like this!" from a stranger, an elderly browser, sitting across from me in a library reading room. It's a little jarring to get the warning sometimes from one you know never allotted the lamented mate a tender syllable while they trod earth together, yet maybe that's the worst regret anybody can have. What many widows and widowers miss most, it seems, is the departed's dependable "thereness," even when it rankled. I can still hear the wistfulness in one woman's "I've got nobody now who's safe to fight with!"

Visiting a pair of widowed roommates, I said with a heartiness that fooled neither of them, "You two women get along so well together, it must be like having a good marriage!" "If you think *that,*" said one, giving me the Myron Cohen eyelid drop, "you must have a damn peculiar arrangement." Well, peculiar or not, should our union go the way of the statistics and Shel is rude enough to check out first, though I like my work, my friends, and even my children, and though I have given him little peace on earth, I'll probably have to fight hard not to join that army of ladies who go around giving younger ones their own warning versions of "enjoy him while you have him"— memento mori. (If *I* should die first, the only thing that worries me about Shel living on without me is that he might find it bearable.)

Auden once wrote that we "must either fall in love / with Someone or Something / or else fall ill." It's true that loving someone or something—one's spouse, a concept of God, an elderly lover who can't quite hear the endearments, the world of ideas, an old fur coat, a special friend—can give people a reason to get out of bed in the morning, even when aching bones send quite another message. But as Auden doubtless knew, one can love any of the above, or invent a love object nobody else ever thought of before, and fall ill and despairing anyway. Still, since there's no mandatory retirement age for the feeling heart *or* for just plain having fun, those who aspire to go into that good night ungently could do worse than to emulate Clara. She's the seventy-four-year-old woman I interviewed who is living it up daily with her beloved in the tub.

Memento mori doesn't mean no bubble baths.

The Latest Wrinkle

There were no bubbles or elderly gentlemen in my tub—
only me—when the phone rang. And though the caller wasn't
an aging admirer, like Clara's, he *was* an old boyfriend, the
dearly beloved of my girlhood. What a surprise! He and I
hadn't spoken to each other, or jointly steamed up a parked
Hudson, since 1947. Back then, he was captain of a wrestling
team and called the Body, a title that so enthralled me in my
teens it seemed reason enough to pledge eternal passion. But
eternity only had a two-year run until the kissing kids got
puckered out.

The Body was between planes when he called me from
O'Hare, and I learned that what with one thing and another,
he had turned fifty and was a classics professor at an eastern
university. I forgot to ask if he was now called the Brain.

"What do you look like?" said the voice that thirty years
ago could shred my huaraches. "I sort of remember that last

time I saw you, you'd just been chosen Sweetheart of something or other."

"Do you remember Maria Ouspenskaya?" I said. "Well, people get Maria and me mixed up. Except her skin has aged a little better than mine."

My old love's laugh was decidedly nervous; he did, indeed, remember the movies' all-time wrinkliest crone. And when I had to break it to him that as a fully accredited middle-aged lady I was unfit for Sweetheartdom of anything (except, with luck, the Gray Panthers), the voice on the line sounded hurt, betrayed. Well, who could blame him? It must be unsettling to turn your back for a second and find that in the meantime, the fresh-faced country girl from whom you coaxed those first warm flushes has moved on to the brink of hot flashes. Professor Body probably wished he could get back the two dimes that had updated him, and I suspected it might be another thirty years between calls.

Despite the jokes, I mind both time's corrosion and my own sensitivity to it. How marvelous it would be to rise above such vanity, a crazy aspiration, as I've admitted earlier, for someone with my Danube-polluted blood. (I know of an elderly Hungarian woman who was all but dead when an intern racing beside her emergency-room-bound stretcher shouted, "Does anyone know how old this lady is?" The life-and-death case raised her head painfully. "Vot," she gasped, "vould you *guess,* dahlink?") But it's not mere frivolity to feel a bit shaken when Time's Wingèd Chariot knocks you down and runs over your face. After all, Nancy Mitford was no bit of fluff, and *she* once wrote ruefully, "I must say, I should very much like to keep my waist, my face more or less having gone already."

My friend Francesca brought hope with her when we met for lunch a year after she'd moved from Chicago. "I bought a face iron!" was her first bit of news. "It's this remarkable little steam thing, you see, and all you have to do is just hold it near your face and press your wrinkles out!"

"Does it work?" I said.

One nostril did a semiquiver. "If it worked," said my pal, "would I look like this?"

Three other women I know, at three different times this year, have pulled back the skin around their eyes and then asked, "Be brutally honest, do you think I ought to have *it* done?"

The *it* that dares not speak its name was a face-lift or eye-bag job, and they were asking whether I thought a bit of nipping and tucking was a tailoring project they ought to consider. (Gather ye rosebuds while ye may is still advice for virgins / For this same flower that smiles today too soon seeks plastic surgeons.) I wish that the reason I get asked such things were tribute to the general quality of advice I'm known to give, but I'm pretty sure that people feel comfortable consulting me about having face-craft done for the same reason we talk about child and marriage problems with those at least as far from perfection as we are. Would you confide in the woman whose worst heartache is that her oldest child can't decide whether to accept the scholarship at Harvard, Princeton, or Yale, that *yours* is joining a cult of pomegranate worshipers? Would you ask Cybill Shepherd whether she thinks your laugh lines are all that bad? Well, now that Ouspenskaya has gone underground, I get asked instead.

There are women, of course, who go in for surgical fixes as casually (and as frequently) as if they were altering an out-of-season hemline. Princess Luciana Pignatelli Avedon, who wrote *The Beautiful People's Diet Book* has been quoted as saying, "Before, during or after marriage, happy or unhappy, I underwent hypnosis, had cell implants, diacutaneous

121

fibrolysis, silicone injections, my nose bobbed, my eyelids lifted.... I will try anything new for beauty." I don't even know what all that stuff *is*, but I read that the princess was also reported to be investigating something called eyelash implants.

Other big-league Beautiful Persons have their buttocks hoisted, as well as surgery that lifts breasts and abdomens (and the contents of one's Gucci wallet). It's their flesh, money, time, and nerve that are on the line, and who's to make judgments? But the people I know who have had cosmetic repairs aren't idle women; one friend did it for the same career reasons many men are flocking to the knife. (At least that's the reason a lot of men give; I think they're just as susceptible, and for some of the same reasons we are.) Nor are these women a light-headed bunch (another friend who's done it is famous for the creases in her brain) or inordinately self-absorbed. They're ashamed, as I am, of minding nature's etchings, and as quick to hang the *N* for Narcissist (or Neurotic) sign on their as-yet unaltered bosoms. They know that compared to sub-Saharan disaster and in the light of feminist advances, sags, bags, and crevices shouldn't mean that much to people. But they're also honest. And if you *do* mind something, what's solved and whose cause is served by denial?

Whatever conflicts people have about such surgery, most share the fear it will hurt in the bank account, what with surgeon's fee, lab tests, hospital stay, operating room, and anesthesia costs. Few, if any, medical insurance plans underwrite what is still considered cosmetic whimsy, although the IRS ruled a few years ago that face-lifts *are* tax-deductible. "I'd do it if I had any money of my own," said Janet, whose grandchild had blurted out, "You were right, Mommy, Grandma *should* have her face lifted up." Janet might have some long-range dependency problems as vexing as her wrinkle ones, but I think she's better off than another friend whose husband was only too happy to pay for her renovation. It was his suggestion, or rather demand, in the first place. There's a great deal of ego difference between being told you need repair work when you didn't *ask* and getting a soul-searched response if you did. The thin line is knowing whether you want your consultant's hard-eyed truth or only some reassuring version of "You've got to be kidding!" Plastic surgeons generally agree that their most satisfied clients are people whose goal is a second turn with their own ten-years-younger faces, and who will be content postsurgery with "My, you're looking well rested" comments rather than "Have you ever considered a screen test?" or "I'll need to see your driver's license, miss, before I can serve you a drink."

Eileen, a woman I know who had a face job at fifty, is straightforward and anything but frivolous. She made no secret of her overhauling, and people tended to react with "If sensible Eileen did it, it must be okay." Eileen herself said, "I was fed up with seeing this tired, depressed-looking woman in the mirror. If I had felt that way, I would have accepted it, but I wasn't tired *or* depressed, and I thought I deserved a chance to look like I feel. Sure, there's some vanity in it. But another word for vanity is self-respect."

She had chosen her doctor after examining the handiwork of various surgeons whom people she knew had used. "I picked this guy because his patients still had real faces, not masks, and he left me with enough lines to look human." Eileen's moment of truth came unexpectedly, not after surgical recovery, but nearly a year later, when her husband had cataracts removed from both eyes. "I realized that he was going to have twenty-twenty vision for the first time in years," she said, "and I was terrified that his first words to me might be: 'What have you done with my wife?' "

Two other women I've spoken to ran out of nerve before the first incision. One of them canceled when the third person in the week before her scheduled surgery told her how young she was looking. "It was the only time in the past ten years I was praying for people to tell me I'd aged," she said, "and you can imagine how shocked a visiting cousin was when she greeted me with 'You haven't changed a bit,' and I said, 'Oh, shut up.' But I did begin to think maybe I was being premature." Another woman changed her mind when she was presented with the release form that absolves hospital and surgeon "in the event of postoperative blindness." Her doctor assured her that in thousands of eye-bag excisions, he'd never so much as dropped a stitch. "But all I could think of," she said, "was, aha! So *this* is how God is going to get me for coveting my neighbor's husband."

People with a flair for guilt can give it a nice workout by way of elective surgery. Ever since my friend Thelma sent the bags under her eyes packing, she has been certain the slightest—or worst—thing that goes wrong in her life is punishment for surgical self-indulgence. I know I'd respond that way, too (which doesn't mean I might not risk it); sometimes I think I'm already being punished for even thinking about such vanities, given what I've learned about life's real disasters (and in the light of disasters that might be practicing their pitches in the bull pen). Well what else *but* divinely directed comeuppance could account for the terrible thing that happened to me on vacation? It was 6:00 A.M. when retribution struck; I remember I was looking my worst after a couple of weeks of nonstop tourist trekking and almost no sleep. We were about to check out of our hotel in Rome; my hair was uncombed, my dress an unwashed and outworn wash-and-wear, my face the worst Roman ruin around. Shel shoved me into the tiny elevator, and I would have slept through the ride down, except I was pushed nose-to-nose to Catherine Deneuve. Has any middle-aged woman ever had a crueler confrontation at dawn's early light? Did my very own husband have to be jammed in the same elevator so that he could get a close-up comparative view, cheek-by-jowl, of Catherine and me—Beauty and the Creased?

But God isn't vengeful full-time. There's a compensatory mercy in another kind of deterioration that often hits about the same time the wrinkles start digging in for good: your eyesight—at least the ability to see things at close range—may start to worsen. And if it does, your skin starts making a remarkable comeback. I am careful not to put my new reading glasses on when I examine the San Andreas fault between my brows, and—what a miracle—it's fading into nothing! But I'll shove those glasses on to stare at a friend who may be looking a little too radiant. Some of my friends stay unfurrowed even under the lens, even at high noon! I think it's impolite of them, if not downright hostile.

There's a Yeats poem called "The Folly of Being Comforted" in which a friend tells the rejected lover not to mind having been turned down since:

> "Your well-belovèd's hair has streaks of grey,
> And little shadows come about her eyes;
> Time can make it easier to be wise
> Though now it seems impossible, and so
> All that you need is patience."

But the spurned one isn't buying easy solace, and he replies that his "well-belovèd" will be even more desirable as she ages, shadows coming and going about her eye liner, "threads of grey" and all, and that "Time can but make her beauty over again!" What a dear man; what a pity there aren't enough like him to go around, sensitive souls who can perceive our beauty when it's coming up—or going down—for the second time. Poets! Well, they'd probably be out there on the campus lecture circuit anyway, telling all the good stuff to our dewy-faced daughters.

Speaking of poets, and writers, perhaps it's well to remember that no one who ever attended an Auden reading was any less stirred because that face was so generously seamed. And how lucky for the reading world that Isak Dinesen had better things on her mind than wishing she were a Danish pastry! She was glorious-looking anyway, her lines a tribute to intelligence and sensibility. Lines *can* be the mark of the life that's been lived deeply, the claims that thought and feeling stake on mortality (or at least the inevitable work of heredity). But if I'd listened when my grandmother begged me not to make so many faces ("Girls aren't *supposed* to be funny"), if I'd spent fewer of girlhood's summers sprawled comatose in the sun so I could strut my hour later as Bronzed Goddess in White Strapless Party Dress, if I'd only learned to get hysterical with a little *restraint,* today I'd be able to risk looking in the mirror with my glasses on to see where my lipstick should go.

What a breakthrough for women it will be when even the most quiescent feminine consciousness is free from such vanities. Maybe, throughout their lives, our daughters and their even healthier daughters will be blissfully indifferent to time's deepest wrinkle (and longest chin hair). I'll bet it's going to be harder to achieve, though, than that warming swell of confidence one gets singing along with "I Am Woman." Illumination may indeed come with true feminist awakening. But Steinem never claimed those golden streaks in her hair were the glow of liberation.

Coming Up Short

About Catherine Deneuve and me in that Roman elevator: I've lied concerning one detail. Part of the reason was to help you visualize my trauma. Mostly, though, I fudged a bit because what happened was even worse. Our confrontation was not quite nose-to-nose, as I described it, but rather my nose to her chest. The truth is that I stand nose-level with very few people who have passed puberty, and when that terrible phrase *little old lady* was invented, it was only being warmed up for my future. In an America dedicated to exercise, diet, and the loss of inches, few people can see the problem of having too few of them. But I can testify that to be a middle-aged woman in a deprived child's body is to be sentenced to the short end of life's stick.

You never grow up if you're short. You may grow old, wise, distinguished, accomplished . . . no matter; people will go on treating you like a not-too-bright child. On your way to get the

Nobel, somebody will offer to hold your hand crossing the street. Somebody *else* will probably ask you if you hadn't better use the bathroom, honey, before you leave for Sweden.

I would have been thrown away by my parents as runt of the litter, but what could they do—I was an only child. Yes, yes, I know; of all the afflictions that genes and nature can deal out, to be a full-grown adult in a deprived child's body is small potatoes, if not just small bones. But the problems can be sizable when *you* aren't. Though Napoleon's analyst maintains a discreet silence, it's well known that the course of civilization might have been different if the elf of Elba had only had as long an inseam as the other guys did, and if Josephine hadn't hinted that there must be more to life than putting hems in the mister's uniforms. The point is, people tend to overreact to those of us who are undersized, and a life of it can make one do strange things. (I wasn't a bit surprised to hear that John Wilkes Booth, at five feet eight inches, was our tallest assassin of presidents.)

Few people understand or sympathize. Take what happened to Eleanor McGovern, for instance, when she was doing the '72 campaign circuit with George. *His* difficulties are history, but how many of us were really aware of what the petite Mrs. McG. had to go through? There was that time in Chicago, for instance, when she was asked to model in a fashion show, along with other wives of prominent personages. Mrs. McGovern was reportedly very polite and quite apologetic; she simply explained that because she had this sort of, well, difficulty with clothes, they probably wouldn't be able to use her as a model. Eleanor, it turned out, was a size three or four (or tops, five). Now did anyone stop to consider what the ramifications of that might be for an adult woman? Did anyone offer so much as a faintly empathetic double tsk? What most of those women were thinking about was not Mrs. McGovern's problems finding things to fit her, but that she could probably eat two desserts, then take darts in the dress she'd worn to her own bridal shower. If they *weren't* thinking that, why would one of them have suggested (at least according to the account I read), "Let's drown Eleanor in the punch bowl"? Yes, and I bet there were a couple of others who would have volunteered to hold that lovely head right under the floating orange slices.

Doubtless some of those ladies thought Mrs. McGovern was just showing off—calling attention to a plight she was crazy about, like the little girl in *Peanuts* who's always reminding everyone of the *burdens* of having naturally curly hair. Well, let me tell you . . . I, too, strain to exceed the five-foot mark and have only gone over 100 pounds on two days in my life, each occasion the day before divesting myself of a full-term baby. So my undersized, overaged heart is all with Eleanor. And I say that if this is a nation that cares about the plight of underdeveloped countries, why can't we do something for underdeveloped women *right here at home?*

The problems worsen as you age, of course, but they get to you early on. I got intimations of my future when I was thirteen and invited to my first dance. Sidney, the young man who asked me, was a cadet at a Pennsylvania military academy; we hadn't met, but his mother knew mine. It appeared that this was going to be Sidney's social debut, too, because he sent me an invitation on which he had written, "The dance will be formal, so please wear a nightgown."

The prospect of shopping for my very first gown sent me into adolescent ecstasies. I turned on the fantasy factory and saw myself dressed in something that would produce instant voluptuousness, if not cover girl contracts. To buy this dreamy number that was to alter my life, amaze America, and enslave the future military establishment, my mother and I made a special trip to Philadelphia; they just didn't have such finery in little Quakertown. But in store after store, saleswomen shook their heads (or turned them to titter in their hankies) when they heard what was wanted, and for whom. My mother began clutching at her heart and panting excessively. And in all of Philadelphia, the only gown that came even close enough to my size for alteration was a flower-girl dress. Or maybe it had been designed for a large baby's christening. The thing was net, with a shirred bodice (that on me looked like a washboard), little puffy sleeves, and net bows strewn all over it—God knows why. My mother said I looked adorable.

Though for weeks before the event, I'd been worrying about what to do if Sidney-the-cadet tried to kiss me after the dance, postball ravishment turned out not to be much of a problem. In fact, nobody (except Sidney, once) asked me to dance. The other girls all had strapless dresses and looked as sophisticated, I thought, as divorcées; I hid out in the ladies' room most of the evening, yearning for death. (I planned to leave a note behind, requesting a closed casket. Otherwise, I knew my mother couldn't be trusted not to have me laid out in that damn baby gown.)

Though I toughed it out to adulthood, shopping never got any easier than the pursuit of that formal. To be a mature woman in America and not of adult-approved dimensions is like living in Vienna with an allergy to whipped cream. I mean, you can look at all those luscious clothes out there, but even if you've managed to squirrel the cash away, the goods are for regulation-sized grownups. Blouses fit like bathrobes, dresses have trains, and everything you put on gives you the sensation that your pants are falling down. (Most skirts and slacks make me feel as I did in those garter belts that used to slide past my hips and allow my first stockings to ring my legs like quoits.)

Women my size can, of course, invade the teen departments, where the pickings are reasonably good for the random sweater, say, or a bra that's only a *bit* too big. But even if your Mantovani- or Mozart-nurtured eardrums can tolerate the volume of hard-core rock in those departments, unless you also hang out at Alice Cooper concerts or junior proms (if the world still has them), the clothes racks offer nothing but rebuke. Besides, when you and your friend's thirteen-year-old daughter are pulling at the same hanger in the same section, you start feeling like one of those awful women who keep cropping up in complaints to Ann Landers. You know the letters. They usually start: "When boys drop in to visit me, my mother comes downstairs in white vinyl boots and a miniskirt and asks them to bugaloo."

Maybe the real reason I became a writer is that you don't need many clothes for it. I lock myself in the house, scribble away, and who cares if the jeans Claudia outgrew at eleven, the skirt I had on the day I got my first period, and a tee shirt Paul wore at Camp Dockrot are my only wardrobe? Creative people, I tell myself, are *supposed* to look different. And if anyone rings the doorbell, I just shout, "There's a small crazy person living here, go away!"

Not that's it's only small women who get short shrift in this country. The fact is that, given two male job applicants with interchangeable credentials, the man who's taller is the overwhelming favorite to get the position (jockeys excluded) according to a study I saw. I've never seen a similar survey about the size / hire ratio for women, but I *do* know that a lot of people tend to treat us as if an undersized brain is the inevitable complement of your cute little body. It's possible I'm also a little paranoid, yet so many petite persons complain of getting the same reaction from taller humans that I don't think there's any doubt; we *do* get a giant share of put-downs, and it didn't start with Randy Newman.

A brilliant middle-aged professor I know—she's author

of several books, and a ninety-pound intellectual heavy-weight—told me that among her male colleagues she has always been treated like someone who would need footnotes to understand Erich Segal. She has had a lifetime of being kept waiting for appointments with dean types (while taller people got punctual receptions), of being fondled by her lessers, and she is all but asked if she needs the letters on the phone dial explained to her.

Then there's trial-by-physician. The male doctor who specializes in patronizing women, though a well-documented pain to patients of all sizes, is at his condescending worst if your stature allows him *really* to look down on you. I'd go right for some of these guys' jugulars, if only I could reach them. I've stopped consulting one—a gynecologist who, when asked how long the tubal ligation we were discussing would take, patted my bangs and said, "Why worry your pretty head about it, little girl? You'll be asleep." I put on the underpants with blue tulips Claudia wore in third grade, and my wee unfettered Fallopians and I went home.

It might be assumed that there are compensations and that small women are blessed with bodily grace. They're a bit younger than I am, but look at Olga Korbut and Nadia Comaneci. And I'm sure that many other of my short-stemmed sisters move like does, too. Well, not me. I stumble about like a moose with a drinking problem. A few years ago I broke a foot by falling over its mate on the tennis court; my first day back I broke an ankle by smashing it on the downstroke of what was meant to be a service ace, thereby becoming the first person at the court where I play who ever tried to serve her own foot. (I *do* have big feet; I'm positively L-shaped. Wouldn't you think that if nature were going to allot me just one large body area, it might have been something I could parlay into cleavage?)

Still, I've had my little revenges, even if the only one I can remember was a bit painful. It happened after I fell down—*all the way down*—a department store escalator, thereby shattering some teeny-tiny riblets. The lift had come off my boot heel; I wasn't sure whether it had got stuck in the store's escalator or had come off during my fall. And because I wasn't sure, I didn't try to collect any damages from the store. "I just don't believe in bringing suit when you might be at fault yourself," I told my friends, with a self-righteousness that had them rolling eyes heavenward behind my battered back.

But my virtue, like my height, only goes so far. So when a month later I got a call from someone identifying himself as an insurance agent who wished to talk to me about "your claim," I said I would allow him to do that. I knew full well I'd never *filed* a claim, but somebody, somewhere, obviously thought I had a case.

Anyway, a baby-boy insurance adjuster—all pink cheeks and curly blondness—showed up, and here's the way I recall our exchange. "Now, Mrs. Wax," said the golden cherub, "I'm going to tape our conversation, so would you just answer my questions in your own words?"

"Okay."

"Now, you realize," he said with awesome seriousness, "I am going to be taping this."

"I do."

"Now then, Mrs. Judith Wax, to whom I'm speaking on February third, 1976, in her living room, what is the worst damage you feel you have sustained from your accident?"

"Well," I said, "before the fall, I was five feet eleven inches . . . and a show girl."

He stared at my stunted body. Boyish lips parted a bit, but no hint of laughter, not even a smile.

"And—um—Mrs. Wax, what do you expect from the company I represent?"

"Well, I know you people will do whatever is fair. I just don't know the actuarial worth of eleven inches. Per inch."

Insurance Lad unplugged his tape recorder and said he'd get back to me. Insurance Lad said he'd better discuss this case with his supervisor. I guess when they heard about my show girl claim back at his office, and the young man described me, they felt they were dealing with brain damage; a quick offer was made to pay my doctor and hospital bills and compensate me for one lost free-lance job. I accepted. But who can deny I was shortchanged, as usual, because here I sit and still not *one* casting call from Vegas.

Meanwhile, my other trials continue. All around me, friends are aging gracefully, acquiring dramatically silvered hair, new poise, a seasoned regality, while I'm still looking for a chair low enough to spare me the indignity of having to sit for the rest of my life with my orthopedic shoes dangling a few inches off the floor. However, I know it would be too much to expect standard-size people to understand the seriousness of these affronts. So let them go ahead with their daily concerns, all those earth mothers, those women who have to beg the world not to regard them as sex symbols, those runners-up all their lives in Sophia Loren look-alike contests. I'll just sit here while my willowy daughter rises taller and taller above me and wait for the worst-yet embarrassment I know is on its way to me. I mean that humiliating day when I will have to whisper to some haughtily statuesque saleslady, "Please ma'am, bring out all your mother-of-the-bride dresses in Toddler Two."

Look, Ma, No Hang-ups

The best thing to do with a daughter who's outgrowing you is ship her out. So Claudia was handed her guitar, and together they went to college. Not long after the willowy one hit the road to higher education, I did, too. I was interviewing women students for another of those "campus mood" articles that are September perennials. The focus of my assignment was sexual attitudes, "What's new?" and "Can it be classified?" variety.

At the Big Ten school I visited first, seven feminists allowed me to sit in on one of their weekly consciousness-raising sessions (provided I promised not to say anything). "Romanticism is the opiate of the oppressed woman," said the Botticelli beauty in combat boots. The others nodded. We were clustered in a little circle, and the kid who raspberried romanticism reminded me so much of Claudia—ethereal and tough— that I suddenly wanted to hug her. Instead, I shifted position to hide my sandaled feet under me. I didn't want the consciousness raisers to notice that my toenails—those running dogs of Revlon—were varnished in Kissing Pink.

But they had better things to do with their emergent awareness and immediately picked up at the place they'd left off last session—exploring their feelings about sex. They ranged in experience, or at least as reported within their little circle, from a tall, shy virgin just beginning to date at twenty to the "Flying Nun" look-alike who'd lost track of the bed count since her thirteenth birthday.

When their mothers were young, maybe they participated in that same sorry ancestor of consciousness raising I did called bull sessions. Bull was an apt name. Or maybe we should have called them cowing-each-other sessions, because in the guise of friends telling the Truth for everyone's greater good, those things were little orgies of hostility, a festival of group-sanctioned bitchiness, an excuse to say mean things— particularly to the prettiest among us.

So what was warming, by contrast, about this little campus circle I audited was the way those young women supported each other, permitted differences. Neither the blithe bed-hopper nor the virgin felt called upon to proselytize, attack, justify. There was a level of acceptance that made room for *real* self-examination and for maybe changing things if you didn't like what the interior view revealed. They could admit failure. Rejection! They seemed, in fact, to have come so far in trusting one another they could even occasionally acknowledge that infuriating gap between theory and the heart's intractability. "I believe total freedom is essential to couples," said the plump one with the little lisp. "So I told my boyfriend my fantasies about sleeping with his best friend. I guess I was sort of trying to get his permission to *do* it, you know? And I kept pushing freedom, freedom and personal growth. But then I got hysterical, I mean out of control, when he admitted he'd let some girl kiss him—*one* kiss—during Thanksgiving vacation!"

Everyone laughed when she said that, a nice little burst of self-recognizing relief. It made me remember my old bull sessions again, when none of us would have dared so human an admission; it was either attack or be gored. But these kids hadn't been conditioned to see one another as threats or each female as potential rival. Why should they? Unlike most of their mothers, they hadn't been packed off to academia as if it were the last husband stop before life's freeway.

Not that everyone who flourishes the sisterhood placard is above smacking you on the head with it. I know a slogan-spouting one-for-aller, thirtyish and single, who has poached on more husbands than Ida Lupino or Barbara Stanwyck in their most predatory screen roles. How does that square, I once asked her, with her declarations of solidarity? "Well," she said, "I sort of decide how advanced their wives are, whether they *deserve* to hang onto their husbands." Since she's rather fond of older men, she manages to find a succession of them whose unemployed and perhaps scantily educated middle-aged wives strike her as unliberated and unworthy and therefore married to fair game. (So much for united-we-stand.)

She is, indeed, a femme fatale in Friedan's clothing, but I'd be surprised if any of the consciousness raisers in the group I visited turn out like her. Though it's hard to gauge, their sisterhood seemed to run deep, and they told me it grew more nourishing with each week's session. What turned out to be the most revelatory thing, though, didn't happen until the day after I sat in with them, when I was telling a college administrator on another campus about some of the feelings they had set off in me. She was a big, breezily confident redhead in an outfit so coordinated that shoes-matched-cardigan-matched-scarf past any expectations you can reasonably have for green. "Look," she said, "I've seen three daughters through college, and what kept 'em in line was fear, sheer fear, and I'm the one who put it into them. I taught my girls if you sleep with a guy, *you marry him.*"

Her assurance was daunting, but I said that I couldn't help thinking while I listened to those young women that if their mothers had been as free to explore life's options, some of those girls would have had different fathers. That is, if they'd been born at *all.* The big redhead's face started to crack like a rock pile loosening. She sobbed, which scared us both, and I could tell this wasn't her standard performance. "That's right," she said, "and if *I'd* known in college that one drunken roll on the floor didn't mean forever, I wouldn't have married their father, that gorilla."

But I'd better watch out for my own smugness; I haven't passed that woman with any great leaps forward in understanding. Even if I can sometimes put names to the shades of my ambivalence, I get confused, too, if not shaken. Maybe the generational remove makes it inevitable that our view of our daughters' world is at best as benevolently blurred as that of a dean of women I heard about. Appointed to her position during the height of campus turmoil, she hoped to anticipate some of the needs of her new charges by remembering her own discontents as a fifties student. That's why one of her first official acts was to order the closets in a dorm under construction be custom-built to accommodate the length and bulk of formal gowns. I can just visualize that woman's trunk when she went to college. Along with the net off-the-shoulder gown, I'll bet—like mine—it included a hat or two for sorority rushing teas. Maybe white gloves. (Claudia was packed for school in three minutes: a thrift shop "fur" coat that could jump into the trunk by itself, some condemned tee shirts, jeans on their last legs, and a bunch of Woolworth's plastic grapes she planned to pin at her waistband for occasions of state.)

Well, so what if we can't comprehend everything? Mothers, as well as that considerate dean of women, deserve points for goodwill, and besides, it makes people nervous to be entirely fathomed. Nevertheless, most of us *do* try to understand, to match our own experience of life's basics with theirs, or at least work out a common language. One woman walked around Chicago for days muttering to herself while she tried to pin down the exact variety of human affection her daughter meant to convey when that Berkeley sophomore phoned to say she wouldn't be home between semesters because she'd met a young man with whom she was, I swear this is true, "in like." (Maybe the Berkeleyite suffered from hyperbolephobia, my husband's affliction.)

But then mothers and daughters have always struggled with linguistics. My mother, in a fit of uncharacteristic avoidance of face-to-face confrontation, once called me from my father's store when I was seventeen to warn, "Your father said to tell you before you go out tonight, there's been entirely *too much necking around.*" That word *around* stuck in there maddened me; who could communicate with such savages? When I went off to college, a roommate and I had long philosophical discussions about which of us had suffered more—I, having to contend with people who said things like necking *around* or she, who had once been debased by maternal counsel against "petting up." My roommate and I agreed that our survival was testimony to the nobility of human endurance in the face of gratuitous adverbs.

Today, although that "petting up" pal is the mother of grown children, she still suffers from problems of generational vocabulary, only now *she's* the mother who says grating things. Funny ones, too, according to her about-to-marry daughter. The imminent bride laughed for a full prenuptial month when her mother suggested time was running out for the two of them to shop for a "going-away suit." It has not escaped my former roommate's attention, however, that the young couple has its own list of "how can anyone get married without it?" requirements. Addicted as they are to Thoreauish declarations, those two advocates of the simple life couldn't embark on their back-to-nature honeymoon trip without L. L. Bean's top-of-the-line matched sleeping bags, ninety-dollar Frye boots, a favored species of imported—and terribly expensive—outdoor cookware. So perhaps brand names have changed, but some people still have de rigueur requirements for the hope chest. ("*Hope* chest?" says my daughter. "*Sick*-o!")

When campus demonstrations had all but died out and there was such a resurgence of sorority and fraternity life reported around the country it began to look possible that those closets for formal gowns might get a workout after all, I started interviewing for another campus story. Its premise was: "Today's college woman is living more like her mother did on campus twenty years ago than like her politically active sister of the late sixties." But I dropped the article when it became clear that only tampered data would make such an idea work. Despite some spurious connections with "the way we were," even sorority presidents, even that anachronism the homecoming queen, even the Deep South beauty contest winner, had ideas about themselves and their lives most of their mothers' generation simply didn't have. It didn't mean all these kids were living in *Ms.*-endorsed ways. But the pull of the women's movement had tugged at expectations everywhere, altered them (though I had a few doubts about that when I happened in on the Ole Miss Campus Queen finals and every second contestant seemed to be competing in the "talent part" by singing "I'm Just a Girl Who Cain't Say No"). Neverthe-less, girls *were* saying no as well as yes in new and relatively confident ways. It seemed clear that young women's assump-tions about marriage, career, children, and their right to pick and choose among those things had traveled such a long dis-tance that even the ones who set their hair every night and wore false eyelashes to class were light-years from mom-as-a-coed.

Like any number of women I know, I find myself cheering our daughters for their advances, for career, educational, sex-ual, and just plain human gains—while at the same time I'm apprehensive about the pressures and complexities they face. I remember a fifties survey of seniors at a top women's college that concluded most of them expected to combine careers, marriage, and motherhood postgraduation. That's what they (and I, and a lot of my friends) said, anyway, but who needs follow-up statistics to know how few of us brought it off? To-day's student often says career comes first, maybe exclusively, an aspiration few of us dared to have and wouldn't have ver-balized. But many other young women say they intend to com-bine career and family. The difference from my generation is most of us *knew* we weren't going to do it, no matter what we told survey makers. We didn't really expect it of ourselves; the people whose judgments mattered to us didn't expect and probably didn't want it for us; our society let us know that it wasn't even a permissible goal (and not worthy of more atten-tion than when we were six and said, "When I grow up, I'm going to be a nurse, a mommy, and a movie star"). The jolt, if it came, was usually in our "empty nest" forties and fifties.

Our daughters, on the other hand, are deadly serious about it all. Most of them are preparing for careers they *mean* to have, though the job market, awed neither by advanced degrees nor by passionate aspiration, may not have *them*.

Their society looks on a woman with a career as more interesting, of more consequence than a woman without one. Though the polite official statement is: "Homemaking is just as important and worthy a choice," few young people today really believe that in the center of their souls.

If there's a man in her life, he probably wants his young girlfriend / wife to have a profession. He probably likes saying, "My old lady's a biologist" (or journalist, or oil rigger). And it's just as likely that despite some beguiling rhetoric, he *also* expects her to be as at home at the kitchen range and as nifty a nest maker as his mother was. His father may have been a chauvinist who didn't let his mother work, but at least the message was clear. In a recent survey of working couples, only a tiny percentage of young husbands were helping their full-time employed wives with so much as a flick of the dust rag.

It's disconcerting that so many college women, when asked how their children will be cared for if they themselves work, refer with vague confidence to "the day care center" as though there were some great amorphous kiddie watcher out there that the state provides. But such places, adequately funded, well run, and available to all, are still scarce in this country, particularly for middle-class women. And figures show that when she takes time off for family-connected reasons (births, child care), a woman's chances for career advancement plummet. In a job market that's steadily tightening and getting more competitive, these obstacles bode the kind of danger ahead that can shatter not only professions, but egos. A hard reality is that there's not much more support for our daughters who have family-plus-career goals than there was for us; there's simply a great deal more self- and societal pressure.

In short, though most of them are better prepared and more determined than we were, the ones who want to juggle marriage, kids, and career aren't getting much practical help keeping the balls in the air. But the emotional stakes are much higher, and what's worrisome is that those who can't manage the balancing act will feel worse about themselves, and what they may interpret as their "failures," than we did. And having expressed those anxieties, I'd still say yes, they *ought* to try for what they want, push for the changes, take the risks. Or what's jumping into life all about? I suspect that they're strong enough collectively to force those changes, and if they don't all make it themselves, at least their daughters (who probably will be cooking up the Home Economics Revival Movement) may have a sturdier system of career supports than they did.

There have been other pressures on seventies college women, of course, and one that seemed to be of universal maternal concern was whether they were being drafted in the sexual revolution before they were ready to serve. Ready or not, some had enlisted with enthusiasm and even had written new combat rules. On every campus, I met a few young women who told me of making quite conscious decisions to choose among lovers as freely (and less seriously) as among courses each semester and without making emotional claims or having any made on them. One Ivy school junior said, "I don't have any sense of moral restrictions, and I don't think there should be any guilt associated with sex. The only time I condemn myself is when I think I've used a person. Like last year, I seduced this guy who was really inexperienced—a virgin, in fact—and I was just out to have a good time. I slept with him before he was ready, without any emotional involvement on my part, and he didn't know how to handle that. I only hope he hasn't been scarred by the experience." ("I'm through with virgins, too," said her friend from across the hall. "I've broken in enough of those guys. I mean you teach them the most fantastic things, and then they go and use them on other people!")

Another coed at a different school, eighteen and a confirmed barhopper who I feared had a Mr. Goodbar future, said, "If someone attracts me just for the evening and I want to sleep with him, I do. And then I'll get out of bed and not think of it anymore. Most people my age want to attach emotion to what they feel is an intimate act; I just walk away." I asked her what attracted her to a sexual partner. "I like slender men," she said thoughtfully, "slim legs and little asses. And I prefer large penises"—here she looked reflective—"although I don't find penises all that attractive. I think you'd probably have to be involved with one person continually to appreciate that sort of thing. What I particularly like is the way skin looks by candlelight. And neck licking. I like music, too," she said, and then the first look of remorse took over that childlike face. "My big regret," she said sadly, "is I don't have a stereo."

She seemed so relaxed and confident, I would have bought what she said—maybe—at face value if I hadn't noted in reading over the transcript of our conversation how many times she referred to her ability to "pick up" people as though it were confirmation of her attractiveness. It made her seem no more emancipated than the girl most of us can remember from our high school days who bought acceptance on her back. Yet another young woman, nineteen and typecast-perfect for a Peck & Peck ad (in my day she would have worn a gold circle pin), radiated confidence as she recalled "oh, gosh, at least thirty sexual partners in the last four years." Perhaps her serenity (and I could easily be mistaken about both these kids) grew out of some sense of continuity that made her less a swinger than an incipient historian. "Sleeping with someone seems like a ceremony," she said, beaming. "I get a feeling of connecting with something that has been done over and over

144

for thousands of years; it's almost a religious ceremony. So many people have done it, but no one does it exactly the same." She reminded me of the line in James Dickey's *Into the Stone* that goes: "The dead have their chance in my body." Her outlook, she said, had "nothing to do with feminism. I'm not political. My independence makes a lot of guys upset and jealous—which has more to do with their egos than with me. I just live the way I *feel.*"

I've talked to a number of young women who—unlike her—did ascribe sexual politics to their personal choices. It didn't mean they'd all chosen one style of behavior, but rather had altered or changed their customary patterns. A few mentioned deliberately cloistering themselves away from male company until they could take, leave, or at least not rely on it. One young woman decided that she could only protect her own identity "by *not* sleeping with the men I love most." She said, "They were usually looking for a monogamous relationship, and if I slept with them, they'd have too much emotion tied up in me. It's better to love some people from a distance, for their good as well as yours."

A Vassar freshman told me, "The woman who plans her life around someone she has supposedly fallen madly in love with is the type of woman who sits around waiting for the phone to ring. I'm guilty of that. I do it a lot! It's really a form of selfishness, anticipating what *I'm* going to get out of a date ... maybe attention, flattery, affirmation of myself as a desirable female. I don't picture men sitting around like that. They probably go about their business and just go out when it's time! Well, I'm working on recognizing that I'm strong! Responsible! Capable!" Having made that resolution, she would—she said—remain a virgin until she got the rest of it right.

Like her, most of the students with whom I talked said

they were taking another look at what some had given wide-eyed, unblinking acceptance to a few years earlier; they were separating fashionable doctrine, other people's pronouncements about "liberated" behavior, from what really felt comfortable. Though a few shared the barhopper and historian's philosophy that personal comfort meant falling into bed as casually and often as they changed knee socks, many agreed with the Bryn Mawr student who said, "We've discovered that the Sexual Revolution was a hype. It had a lot of us jumping into bed without resolving some of the basic conflicts. I learned I can't handle one-night stands, and that I have romantic and emotional needs as well as sexual ones." "Romanticism is the opiate of the oppressed woman," the students in that little consciousness-raising group would have warned her, while other young women—like the kid who looked ready to dash down a hockey field—were fighting monogamous impulses. "You could call me a one-penis female," she said. "The one-penis female is a product of guilt and insecurity, who can only enjoy a man's body if she has emotional feelings. Sex is the ultimate enjoyment, and I know instinctively that it shouldn't be restricted to the emotion of love, but unless there's a tremendous feeling of reciprocity, I feel like a tramp. I enjoy sex more and put more of myself into it when I'm in love." Still others announced unabashedly, "It has to be special, I have to be in love to sleep with someone," even though some of these confessed to doing a "this is the real thing" hard sell on themselves that had a familiar ring for someone of my vintage. (I was surprised at how many young women claimed that monogamous relationships were of less importance to them than to the men they knew, although several ascribed it to the fact that "the guys around here are so busy trying to get into graduate school they want one steady woman around so they don't have to take up their precious time pursuing people.")

A Yale undergraduate expressed a sentiment I heard often. Though she had been devastated by love gone wrong in her sophomore year, she still felt that an "intense, one-to-one commitment" was the best, most satisfying arrangement. "And despite the pain it caused me, if I don't eventually love and find someone who loves me, there will be a lot missing in my life," she said. But she made it clear she had no intention of languishing until the big passion showed up again. "Good caring sex with a good caring friend can be very special, very satisfying and not really 'casual' sex at all—although that's what a lot of people call it. And I've evolved a formula I feel comfortable with that goes: If you wake up next morning and you don't feel guilty, it was probably good for you."

At some schools she spoke in a whisper, but the voice of the virgin was still heard saying no in the land. "They call me the iceberg here," one told me. She'd been engaged for several years and said that when she married, lights-off, missionary-position sex would prevail in her household. Another, a Northwestern sophomore, said, "I'm happy, comfortable about it, and sometimes guys tell me, 'As much as I hassle you, I really don't want you to change.' In the long run a lot of them want this sweet little innocent wife only *they've* slept with. But one thing I think about is, what if I die before I've done it?" Many said they just hadn't met "the right person" or had the right opportunity, and a number of students at Ole Miss explained, like one Delta belle, that "if you hold out till you get married, sex probably won't get boring so fast." But no matter where the young women I interviewed were on the scale of sexual experience, what seemed strikingly different from my own days on campus *and* the late sixties was a growing feminine

147

confidence in the right to listen to your own body and brain, march (or lie down) to your own sexual drummer, and even call the tune.

"This is the healthiest group of women, emotionally, that we've seen," one college psychologist told me. But her colleague on the next campus said, "We're seeing more women now who internalize and worry about themselves too much. During the days of political activism, those kids could work out their anxieties by protesting them off." And at yet another campus, the director of psychological services said, "Mothers are always telling me, 'I'm worried that my daughter can't handle what goes on around her, like her roommate making love in their room, for instance.' I tell them, 'Sure, some kids *have* been upset by things like not being able to sleep in their own beds because of the action in the next one. But there are more serious emotional problems in this place caused by people blasting their stereos!' " ("I'm so miserable that I cry myself to sleep every single night," a sorority beauty told me, "and my mother is sure that I'm just like she was, crying about sex and men. But that has nothing to *do* with it. I'm just terrified that after all this work I won't get into grad school!")

If our college daughters were beginning to blow the whistle on outside ownership of their bodies, they were also—I found—putting new limits on what chemicals and contraptions they were willing to put into them. The diaphragm renaissance was in flower. A Haverford senior echoed sentiment I heard at every school but Ole Miss. "What kind of liberation is it to put a pill that could be a time bomb in my body," she said, "just so I'm always ready at someone else's whim or convenience?" There was growing resentment, too, over male-dominated funding and research for new birth control methods ("They wouldn't put that stuff in their *own* bodies"). And there were plenty of horror stories about blood clots, pain, pill-

148

happy health services that prescribed—or so I was often told—as if women were riskable percentiles and resisters merely unreasonable.

Perhaps my generation of mothers has been dangerously, irresponsibly silent. Whether we approved or didn't, we *knew* what the figures said. We knew that many of our daughters were sexually active at least some of the time, and I haven't met anyone who was yearning for premature grandmotherhood. Yet where was our strong collective voice pressuring for safe, easy, economical birth control for ourselves and those daughters, married or not, who have been walking test labs for a variety of chemicals, metals, and assorted foreign objects that did some of them instant harm and who knows what long-term damage? Too bad we didn't yell on their behalf or along with them.

Maybe it's also regrettable that research on a particular oral contraceptive intended for males was abandoned when it was discovered the users' eyeballs turned red (another pill for males was rumored to make the skin go bluish in sunlight). What more effective birth control test could there be than to look a perspective partner in the eye and be able to certify his safety (or note the Blue Boys for future reference)? Okay, I'm not serious—not quite. But I cringe in the face of what we have yet to learn of chemical fallout, as I am sickened remembering the women of my generation who were advised to take DES to prevent miscarriage and lived to see their offspring develop cancer twenty years later—the legacy of the drug that "saved" their children. I'm not suggesting men should be subjected to chemical danger by way of contraception, either. However, there has to be some equity, some sharing of physical and emotional responsibility. It was funny—and also rather sad—when a young woman at that consciousness-raising session said, "My definition of a true gentleman is a guy who'll wear a rubber if you ask him to." And everyone present agreed (though some had never actually *met* such a gentleman).

"The division between male and female has hurt the female in the past," said a Yale senior, "and one way to reconcile it is to move toward androgyny. I don't know how far it will go, but if everyone ends up bisexual, that might be good. I think that most people are basically bisexual, and I hope there can be equal feeling and satisfaction as in heterosexual relationships. There is a real bisexual alternative. Lesbianism may be a necessity on an immediate level, as a means of change."

For some parents I know, the one midlife crisis they hadn't expected to face was confronting an offspring's newly announced homosexuality. "I could accept it," said one mother, "if I thought my daughter were responding to biological pressure. What bothers me most is my suspicion that lesbianism is something she's heard and read her way into. Or that she sort of drifted into it before she had enough heterosexual experience—or at least *good* heterosexual experience—to have developed a real sexual identity." It's true that I interviewed students who were as apologetic for not having "tried it yet" as if they were confessing racism or not having read the year's big book on campus. But the fear of not being *au courant* was most memorable in a seventeen-year-old freshman, an Alice in Vassarland who didn't look much past Sesame Street (and had yet to have her first sensuous encounter of the mildest variety). "I know people are supposed to be open to any human experience," she told me, "but I just don't think I'll ever be able to do anything, you know, sort of funny with animals." Whereas a kid in the same dorm said that though she wasn't intrigued by bestiality, either, she'd tried just about everything else with both genders, most apertures, and in multiples. "Kinky sex," she said, "is like a Marx Brothers comedy." However she, too, had her limits. "I once did an

S/M thing with a guy. I tied him up," she explained, "but I wouldn't hit him. So we compromised. I poured hot chicken soup on him."

I found no other soup experimenters, and no animal acts, thank God; if such things ever went on at the places I visited, people were too considerate to tell it to the nice middle-aged lady. But many students *are* homosexual, and they are neither victims of modish literature nor anyone's recruitment campaign. The reasons aren't clearly understood, and no one has proved homosexuality to be psychic malfunction. Each decade produces more "experts on the subject," but little hard information. One of the more thoughtful remarks I heard was made by a Yale student, herself heterosexual, who said, "We saw a documentary film that showed two male homosexuals making love, and you could see that they cared about each other and were taking time to make each other feel good. They were open and romantic and gentle, and *that* turned on the women who were watching the film. In heterosexual relationships, if more men could understand that sensitivity doesn't undermine their male sexuality but enhances it"—her comment reminded me of how many young women said the best part of being in bed was "good talking"—"they'd be a lot more attractive to women."

"At first it was terrible for me to accept," said one friend about her youngest daughter. "But I started thinking that if she really is a lesbian—what do I mean, *really?*—she *is*—then we're all damn lucky she's living in an atmosphere where she doesn't have to hide, or kill herself like a girl I knew at school did, or live without expressing love. I know when she graduates, there will be plenty of people in the world quite eager to provide her with anguish, but she won't get any of it from me." Another woman said, "I wanted the fact of her homosexuality to go away, but not *her*. So I began to examine my feelings, bit by bit as I could handle them. And now I'm almost at the place where I think I can either approve or disapprove of the women in her life by the same standards, if things had turned out as I once expected, that I would have applied to husband candidates." (I suppose both those women would have stunned the couple I recently read about who, when informed of an offspring's homosexuality, held a public prayer meeting.)

Maggie Kuhn, the seventy-four-year-old leader of the Gray Panthers, said in a Los Angeles speech, "Considering the demography and the imbalance between men and women in the older population, we have to think of new kinds of arrangements. I daresay, at the risk of the house falling in on me, that maybe for older women some kind of lesbian relationship may be encouraged." Perhaps younger women, in their generally more accepting attitudes toward human sexuality, including lesbianism, are showing us the wave—or at least a ripple—of the future for older women. And my generation will probably have to keep scrambling to comprehend the changes in the generations on either side of us.

Yet maybe our struggle to accommodate has been more flexible and understanding than our children's attitudes toward *us,* at least as far as sex is concerned. A 1977 *Psychology Today* survey noted college students' evaluations of their parents' sexuality, and according to most of our kids, we don't have any. Or nothing worth mentioning. The student consensus was something like: "My parents, if they make love at all, do it rarely, joylessly, unimaginatively, and—in the past—only to produce the likes of me." Doubtless some of them were right, but others may just have been responding petulantly to what fun they suspected we were having without their inhibiting and distracting presences on the home front. Wherever truth (or passion) lies, our kids—despite their comparative sophistication—probably need to deny parental sexuality as we did (and still do) and as children have always done.

But with all the human potential movement vocabulary and goodwill parents and children can muster, some primordial taboos remain, and maybe it's wise to keep liberating hands off them. (Or, if you must hack away at deep-rooted prohibitions, make sure you don't faint at the sight of blood.) A brilliant, articulate freshman told me, "My mother is informed and intelligent, and we're very close, except that when I try to talk frankly to her about my sex life, I can tell she's gritting her teeth. She just doesn't want to hear it, and her attitude really upsets me."

I asked her whether if her mother were having an affair, she would like to hear the details of *that*. She recoiled as if I'd hit her, covered her ears, and all but slid under the sofa. Although a girl at another campus said she'd be hurt if she *didn't* share her mother's experience, this young woman's aversion was so automatic that she and I both learned something about the depth of certain human reticences. Still another student said, "I'd absolutely flip out if I knew my mother was having an affair. That's *adultery*; how can you compare it with sex before marriage? But then, maybe I have to say to myself that my mother has the same gut reaction to sex before marriage for *me* as I have when it comes to adultery for *her*."

Even the most loving mother-daughter communication sometimes gets garbled. But I doubt any mother has been more mystified by her daughter than one student was after a sex talk with *her* mother. The daughter, twenty-one, was a huge-eyed waif at a Catholic women's college another junior described as a place where "the virgins and nons—the cool and uncool—sit at separate dining tables." She was dressed in an army surplus coat that nearly hid her from sight, though she gave off nearly visible bursts of indignation, as she sputtered out the tale of her mother's "strange behavior." "I told my mother what oral sex is," she said, "and you're not going to believe this, but she'd never heard of it. Married twenty-five years, five kids; I said to myself, 'What the hell were we, virgin births?' My mom said, 'Oral sex?' with this huge question mark hanging there. You can imagine that I was almost in tears; this was *my own mother!* I said, 'Please, Mother, tell me you know what I'm talking about.' She said she didn't. I said, 'Mother, oral . . . you know, *mouth.* And your hand sometimes, too.' She said, 'Oh, um, what do you do with the uh—?' I said, '*Swallow* it, mother!' She didn't dream it all had anything to do with me, of course; I was simply the college girl passing on information."

This particular information-dispensing college girl had collected such a firsthand fund of it by her junior year that if her mother had heard a few of those adventures, the woman might never have swallowed again, let alone learned new esophageal tricks. Or she might, like one distraught mother I heard about, have written anonymous threatening letters to every young man she suspected her daughter of sleeping with, a gesture which exhausted the woman's stationery supply, but not her energetic offspring.

Well, what's a nervous mother to do? There's a sign at a deer enclave in Nara Park, Japan, that reads: "CAUTION! Everybody: take care of Hind! It is the season Fawn is born about this time. It may be the case, if you approach fawn the mother, being full of maternal love gives you a kick by her forefeet." A mortal middle-aged mother can (as the young say) "relate to" that sign. Being "full of maternal love"—and sometimes fear and neurotic churnings—we want to do some of that kicking at the dangers, just like those protective Japanese deer. The problem is recognizing which are the dangers. Sure, some of our campus kids are in questionable shape, if not cultural calamities. What generation hasn't produced its own quota of the wounded and the foolish? But touring campuses, as I did, you get a reassuring feeling that most of our daughters are equipped to spot danger before we could have done it for them and are pretty adept at kicking by their own forefeet.

Not that I claim clinical detachment in this area (or any other). How can I, when sometimes I cried at the sad stories, like the one I heard from the freshman seduced by a married professor twice her age? "He probably ignores me now because he's afraid he has fallen in love with me, don't you think?" she asked. "Or maybe it's because I *tried,* but I really wasn't very expert at those fellatio and cunnilingus things because I was a virgin, you see; in fact, I haven't even dated much." And I once took a kid twice my size in my lap while we both wailed over her betrayal and who knows what ancient unhealed bruise of my own.

I've worried a bit that some of the young women I met were striding past a few lovely things. They've almost *all* missed the possibilities in close-up dancing, and I hate to think that any might throw out tenderness, learning to wait, heart-pounding anticipation, the hard demands and big rewards of loyalty (and even occasional silliness) along with life's *real* garbage. But that's all subjective, and besides, who can trust a woman who still gives valentine parties?

I found some endearing throwbacks. There was the senior on a midwestern campus who'd had the same boyfriend for eight years and had been sleeping with him for most of that time. "But I won't take a shower with him," she told me. "We haven't held back on anything else, so I want to save *that* till we're married." And I will love forever the no-nonsense radical feminist I met in '74 who was missing from the protest meeting when her turn came to give a report because she'd sneaked home to watch Rhoda's wedding on TV.

I have known mothers my age who sailed through each

adjustment and coped placidly with all manner of contemporary challenge only to snap, crack, and go berserk over a daughter's body hair. I saw an unflappable—I thought—mother of five disintegrate at the sight of her eldest's legs revealed in tennis shorts for the first time in years. "You look like Billie Jean Bushman!" she shrieked. Another friend said *her* darkest moment came when her daughter—who usually spurned such elitist dunkings—appeared for a swim at the country club one summer afternoon. "I was sitting at the pool with some people," said my friend, "when Polly floated by in an inner tube, face up, hands locked behind her head, and her underarms trailing hair a foot behind her. As *she* used to be so fond of saying, it was the pits!" I've also known husbands and wives who have lived through fifty-seven varieties of trauma and still have the energy to stay up half the night imploring each other, "*You* tell her to shave," "No, *you!*"

We nuclear families bump along hoping for understanding, and it's sometimes surprising when we get actual glimpses of it. Lots of us astounded ourselves by our adaption to, if not endorsement of, our children's campus and postcampus living arrangements. We could, it was discovered, sometimes even grow downright fond of a common-in-law, though what to call that person (say, during an introduction) remained perplexing. For most people, the stickiest moments came when roommates were brought home on a visit to share the very bed once limited to partnership with a teddy bear or the family dog. And if you worked *that* out, what did you tell your own elders? One woman I know wanted to protect her aging mother and father from learning that their adored granddaughter had begun living with a boyfriend, but when prodded for the name of the "young lady" her daughter was sharing the new apartment with, my friend got flustered and said, "Inez"—the name of the young couple's cat. Pressed further for a last name (and addicted to truth), she sputtered, "Feline"—giving it an Italian pronunciation, which led the grandparents to ask whether this roommate might be related to the famous movie director.

Well, each generation copes as best it can. When I used to bring dates into the family living room after my parents had gone to bed, my mother would take so many round-trip excursions to the bathroom overhead that the unrelenting mood music of her flushings would de-eroticize the juiciest adolescent. On the other hand, it was progressive of her not to make a personal appearance. When *she'd* brought young men home, her father would march into the living room—his teeth still in a glass upstairs—point to the door with one hand, and hold his inevitably stringless pajamas up with the other while she trembled that he might open his mouth or, worse yet, let go.

My mother-in-law, for her part, wasn't all that relaxed about my sharing her son's old bed even after we were married. In fact, our union had been legitimate for several months when we spent a weekend visiting his parents and came downstairs our first morning there to find the groom's mother radiating disapproval.

"What's the matter, Mom?" her only son asked.

"I couldn't sleep a wink last night," she said. "Do you realize that when you people went to sleep, you closed the door?"

We stared at her, sure of our guilt, but not yet certain of the offense's name. "For heaven's sake!" she exploded. "You two could have *smothered* in there!"

They Don't Make Sex
Like They Used To

Journalists didn't bother much about stalking campus moods and sexual attitudes when I was a student. Maybe it was assumed that *nice* kids didn't have such things, though I would have been happy to bare my mind for the asking. But to have plumbed my knowledge of the body and its possibilities would have netted as much firsthand information as a list from Jackie Onassis of Twenty Ways I've Learned to Stretch My Budget. In fact, if some of the students I've interviewed for one article or another had turned the tables and asked about my own sexual attitudes when the world and I were young, I'd have been hooted off this nation's quadrangles quicker than you can say premature ejaculation.

Not that I wasn't as dogged as Nancy Drew, pursuing the mysteries of being female from the time I suspected, on the flimsiest evidence, that's what I was. My goal was to organize myself into something called a typical teenager, and toward that end I bought a thirty-seven-cent "Mairzy Doats" record, a "broomstick skirt" you stored wrapped around the wooden handle that came with it, Tangee lipstick (Natural), and socks with metal clip-on initials that gave me a J-shaped ankle infection. I also bought a "friendship ring" made of two clasped hands, one of which was supposed to be disengaged and given to a beloved. Half of *mine* was meant for either John Garfield or Dane Clark, whoever showed up in Quakertown first. I hounded my parents into buying me a dressing table covered by three tiers of ruffled organdy on the theory that sitting in front of such feminine flounce would transform me into the glamorous older sister in *Junior Miss*. Who cared that she was portrayed as a shallow bit of baggage? She was beautiful, the book said, and popular, and I had enough troubles without trying to develop character, too.

In swift succession, I fell in love with a boy at camp named Penrod Schmeer, then a camper named Beanie because I'd never before seen a thirteen-year-old with a middle-aged pot-belly. That paunch was such a precocious achievement that I thought it lent maturity to my feelings for him. But Beanie's bulge was quickly forgotten when I got back to Quakertown and met a boy who, or so my friends whispered, had done time in reform school. Even criminal *thoughts* were unheard of then in my innocent hometown, and I sensed that, in this persona, John Garfield had come for me at last. When the alleged kid con sauntered onto our porch one afternoon—as I'd dreamed he would—he lifted one pant leg to show the still-bloody and very pulpy place a horse had just kicked him. The sight made me giddy with ardor, but he disappeared (back to stir, someone said) and didn't even write.

Because my grin showed too much gum, my grand-mother—who had me confused with Gigi—conducted smiling seminars after school. She enlisted pretty Aunt Ruth to show me how to "get any boy interested in you" by a Magyar-tested technique of rolling and batting one's eyes. I crossed mine, instead, and mugged, so my relatives gave me up for a bad job and predicted the only male who ever would share my Saturday evenings would be Snooky Lanson.

It was a time when I knew my own undersized body like I knew the intricacies of King Hammurabi's law code. I "took piano" for years longer than either my teacher or I could stand my playing because there were Kotex ads (with quizzes!) in some magazines he kept in his waiting room. Then, when I couldn't recruit anyone into the Calling All Girls Club I tried to start, I threw myself on the mercy of the Girl Scouts in a last-ditch effort at finding out what other girls knew. An only child is often the last to learn life's basics, and when the women in my family had something interesting to say in my presence, they switched to speaking in tongues—German or Hungarian.

Joining Troop Ten promised breakthrough at last, because before my first tenderfooted month was up, a couple of girls invited me to join their postmeeting soda cadre. But when Elsie Schmoyer whispered to us that her older sister Dotty "fell off the roof" that very week, I gasped and asked if Dotty had been injured. So even though I played my piano solo, "Moonlight Cocktail," with a great deal of feeling at the next Scout talent show and wore a garland of artificial flowers in my braids to look like Esther Williams at the Scout Swim (the color came out in the water and dyed my hair orange), no one let me in on anything significant again. I quit, uninformed, depressed, badgeless.

Just when I was considering hanging myself by my undershirt as the only honorable way out, my mother let me have a slip with real straps, narrow ones. Then I wangled a sort of filmy blouse to wear over it. It was my way of making sure everyone in seventh grade noticed those little metal strap adjusters on my shoulders, epaulets for the only rite of passage I could book space on.

In the forties, training bras were a rotten idea whose time had not yet come, yet they would have spared me having to stitch so many alterations in the brassieres I stole from my father's ladies' apparel store that I looked much more corrugated than curvesome. I *yearned* for anatomy, with all its attendant effluvia. But I was unconscious to the borders of coma about its details.

Nora Ephron, in her book *Crazy Salad,* wrote that she faked menstruation before it was a fact of her life. Maybe feigning menses is a form of writer's cramp, because I did the same thing, putting on great shows of pain on what the *As One Girl to Another* pamphlet called "those certain days," arriving late to class, then sitting down with ostentatious care and even little grimaces of pain when I was sure everyone was looking. For one whole camp season, I bought so many unnecessary sanitary napkins I could have used them to rebuild Bunk Five as an igloo. But after all that sham and rehearsal, here's how I reacted to the real thing, according to an entry in my eighth-grade diary:

> *March 18, 1945.* I had blood on my underpants today and I cried because I thought when I fell at gym I must have broken my backside. Mother is in Florida so Aunt Ruthie told me what really happened and gave me advice. She said, "Never talk about cramps with other girls it is very boring conversation."

My diary also reveals, a few years later, that if mononucleosis were really the kissing disease (as it used to be called), I got off easily with only a single two-month seizure. Initiated into "necking," I found it highly absorbing stuff, and a few times I could have sworn I heard music, just as those pink and yellow song sheets with all the popular song lyrics in them had promised. But despite random gypsy violins, no glandular rush propelled me into upping the erotic ante—at least not for years. A friend says that when we were teens, boys like him invented the great myth of "blue balls" to help them in the seduction of the tenderhearted. (The first time I heard the expression, I thought it referred to a sort of flower.) I like to think my friend is right, that the term was an exaggerated metaphor. If not, my generation's marathon neckers created their own coast-to-coast species of lapis lazuli.

Still, there are those who think that our country's young could profit by a rerun of such forties diversions. The Reverend E. Spencer Parsons, dean of Rockefeller Chapel at the University of Chicago, once told me during an interview, "That old American institution of petting was a great one, a healthy way for our generation to get to know each other sexually without being vulnerable to the consequences of coitus." (As a leader in Clergy Consultation Service and an early advocate of legalized abortion, the Reverend Parsons is more than passingly familiar with the coital consequences of which he speaks.) "Our generation could enjoy each other as persons and bodies," he said, "without being hung up on intercourse and the number of orgasms we could somehow manipulate simultaneously."

Maybe some of those women I interviewed who had first affairs after years of monogamy were simply expressing nostalgia for girlhood's pastimes. A lot of us went straight from backseat kissing to the altar. I know a woman who tried to bribe her husband into necking in the car, "like we did in college, Charlie," by promising a few unspecified but exotic additions they hadn't ventured in the old days. Charlie said, "Police!"

Such things, at any rate, were the popular entertainments in pre-TV Quakertown. And though I kissed away my high school years with diligence, I didn't come up for air much better informed than when I was in Troop Ten. Once an enterprising date guided my hand over his pants to the rigidity beneath, a maiden's voyage that convinced me the male organ must look like one of the grayish purple necks my grandmother was always yanking out of raw chickens.

By the time I married, after two years of "going steady," I had pretty much nailed down the essential differences between a man and a Rhode Island Red. The wedding was held a few weeks after my twentieth birthday (Shel was twenty-four), and I'd also mastered everything you had to know about honeymoons. I knew, for instance, that they didn't let you have one unless the bride owned a peignoir; just *saying* peignoir seemed the height of voluptuary pleasure. The groom wore maroon, shiny pajamas that spent the next three years at the bottom of our hamper. Their tag said "Hand Wash Separately," a nicety I never managed before the lease was up on our first apartment. His mother had also given him honeymoon bedroom slippers, with innards that glowed in the dark like the feet of a tiny moon visitor. They were very practical; if he'd ever thought it necessary to make a middle-of-the night escape from wedlock, he could have located his slippers before the first cold germs mobilized.

The fact that the only two months in my whole reproductive life—so far—that I wanted to get pregnant, I did (and didn't when I didn't) is dazzling. Well, dazzling given an anatomical ineptitude not so unusual at the time. (One honeymooning friend had to telephone her gynecologist long distance for step-by-step instructions every time she wanted to remove her diaphragm.) When Shel and I decided the world would be a better place once we contributed our issue to it, I experimented with the body temperature method to pinpoint the fertile days. The first time I tried it, though, I got scared and called my friend Sheila, who had put me onto the technique in the first place. "What do you do if the thermometer breaks in there?" I asked her. "Isn't the mercury dangerous?"

"In *where*?" Sheila said, and straightened me out when I told her. I'd imagined you had to regulate your temperature *in situ,* like preheating an oven. Doing a headstand afterward was my own fecundity ritual and meant to direct sperm traffic—like some wee dumb Chinooks—properly upstream.

Over the years, I did manage to become a lot more familiar with the body's terrain; when you're a short person, there's less to memorize. My friends tell similar stories of bodily incompetence (which a lot of us saw as good manners), and—happily—it would be hard to find our counterparts in naiveté among young women today. But occasionally I get an uneasy feeling that in the great leap forward, some of the excitement of discovery got trampled to death. You can take such a clinical, direct, and no-nonsense approach to sex that it's also no-fun. And though it's true that the mainstream of sexual advice runs to "relax, enjoy, and don't count orgasms" counsel, an impression lingers on of some ghostly expert standing by the bed with a digital computer.

There's no doubt that my generation as well as my mother's could have benefited vastly from today's general loosening up and availability of information. There are sexual self-help articles in nearly every magazine at nearly every checkout counter, and they're often written with such how-to-proceed clarity that they make the diagram in a box of tampons look like directions for making DNA at home. The catch with some of these articles is that in their fondness for terms of instruction like "doing your homework" (masturbation) and "the next assignment" (enlisting someone to rub you with baby oil) they can give you a feeling you're learning more about pant-by-numbers than ecstasy. For instance, I came across one self-help piece that charted a day-by-day, week-by-week plan for heightening sexual response through familiarity with your own body. It was meant to help women overcome problems of orgasmic dysfunction, a worthy goal and who would quarrel with it? But reading those instructions, you can get the disquieting feeling that if getting to know yourself isn't a little more fun than that, maybe you'd rather not be introduced.

This was basic Week One strategy: every day, for one week, look at your genitals in a mirror. For one hour each day. Now there's no question that she who considers her genitals repulsive, shameful, or second-class members needs attitudinal alteration, or maybe a bath. (I believe bidets ought to be an everyday American plumbing option, even though the one woman I know who owns a bidet—hers is red porphyry like Napoleon's tomb—only uses it to wash her feet.) Many women of my age can be grateful to younger ones for leading the way toward self-acceptance, even though most of us will never feel really relaxed with such refinements as the speculum buddy system. A lot of women learned late that what they grew up uneasily calling "down there" is really a nice place. Shakespeare's term was "a nest of spices," and a freshman I once interviewed said proudly, "The vagina is self-cleaning, you know." (She apparently had the same fixation on oven imagery I did twenty-three years earlier with my "fertility thermometer.")

Back to the Plan for Week One, however, and the daily crotch watch. Now heightened sensuality and correcting orgasmic reluctance are first-rate objectives. But one hour every day of mandatory staring could make you feel you were eight years old again and told to sit quietly through *The March of Time* because it would do you worlds of good. I think when you get the hang of staring (there could be an honor system) by whatever day it took, they should let you get up and read Colette or Nadine Gordimer or Jean Rhys to learn some other things about being a woman, or at least be dismissed early so you can go downstairs and start the soup.

Or why not just begin Week Two before the other pupils? Though that was the week you moved on to basic masturbating, again for the requisite one hour every day for seven days, there were still no concessions to the quick study. There wasn't even a hint about what to do in case *you're* finished before the hour is. In *Life Signs,* a sad and funny novel by the late Johanna Davis, the protagonist says that she's ashamed to admit to her psychiatrist that she has never masturbated. She's not, she confesses, even quite certain where to find her own clitoris, an oversight she ascribes to never having had "to do anything for herself which somebody else could be found to do for her." Now I can really identify with that; it's the reason I've never learned to change my own typewriter ribbon.

Still, it's obvious that character and I both need to unjell our mind-sets, so on to Week Three. There's a danger by this time (the article didn't mention it) that if you've been following the previous weeks' schedule, you may have been locked in your room for so long people have forgotten you. But if you can still scare one up, this is the week for a partner to get into the act. Or acts. The problem is I can't remember exactly what they *are* or what the instructions were beyond this point (and for all I know I'm the last woman in this country who can't play the marimba with a dildo). I stopped reading, not because I couldn't use erotic instruction. No, indeed. It's just that if there's one thing I've always hated, it's knowing exactly where I'm going to *be* every day.

As for America's vibrator explosion, I'm not much of a reporter on that front, either. I don't even know anybody who uses one—or who talks about it, anyway. But then I didn't have much chance for ecstasy *ex machina*; my mother still warns me that people get electrocuted if they bathe during a lightning storm. Or keep the radio on.

When your own experience is limited, sometimes you have to rely on the testimony of strangers, such as the gentleman who wrote to a magazine's letters column to share his discovery of bliss beyond vibrator. He and his wife, he reported, had found something much better, and not only did the earth move, their whole condominium trembled when he stuffed the lady with scarves (he recommended top-quality silk ones) and slowly disengaged them. Perhaps when the scarves weren't in play for peak sex, she tied them into that little sling for one's bottom certain stylish ladies began wearing over skirts and slacks a few seasons ago.

It's hard to judge that couple's standing on the scale of looniness without knowing how old they were. Sexual perceptions, like so many other things, often depend on generational vantage point, and while we may perform the same acts (forget scarf tricks) with comparable, if older, equipment, we sometimes invest those acts with different meanings. A friend who is my age and a late-starting playwright was dazed by such perception differences when she went to a read-through of one of her plays. She is a gentle soul and her play, its wit, and its heroine (who exclaims, "Oh, fiddle!" as her creator sometimes does) are all gentle, too. But the acting troupe getting the feel of my friend's comedy to "see how it plays" was accustomed to stark, very contemporary confrontation drama and the director and cast were considerably younger than she was.

The main communication problem centered on a goat, whose dramatic significance—other than as laugh getter—was to point up the heroine's kindhearted vagueness. The animal had followed her home, and rather than confess having given it asylum in their basement, she explains the occasional offstage bleatings to her stuffy husband as "trouble with the furnace, dear."

During the run-through, my friend began squirming when it became apparent that the young woman playing the *Voice of the Turtle*-ish heroine was interpreting the character as though she'd sprung from the head of Albee. But the actress was conscientious about her craft, and afterward, in pursuit of motivational purity, she cornered the gentle, middle-aged playwright. "Is the woman I play actually making it with the goat?" the young actress inquired. "Or is she just bringing him off by hand?"

Though it's possible to share a great deal with a younger friend, even an age difference that seems inconsequential can suddenly become a chasm that leaves you standing on either side of it, staring at each other. A younger friend of mine is unmarried by choice and elected, in her thirties, to have and raise the baby when she became pregnant. ("It's now or never," she said, "and I don't want to miss the experience of motherhood.") I wouldn't presume to judge the wisdom of that, but I was pleased to be invited to a large shower given a few weeks after the baby was born, and flattered to be included among so many younger women who must have recognized (I told myself) my "young attitude," my flexibility. I was not, it turned out, flexible enough to jump the gap. I understood perfectly well the huge problems she faced in raising and supporting a child by herself and as an unmarried career woman/mother in a society not yet geared for such an arrangement. But as I watched her opening that undiminishing pyramid of baby gifts, the increasing worry I felt for her had nothing to do with the realities of her life and everything to do with what I'd once learned were the essential issues. Luckily, everyone at the shower thought my question was meant to be funny. "How will you *ever* manage to cope," I asked nervously, "with all the thank-you notes?"

Once Shel, too, nearly got a hernia trying to leap the age chasm. It happened the summer afternoon we were the only middle-aged couple invited to a party a group of younger married couples whom we barely knew gave at a farm they'd rented in the country. We congratulated ourselves (I'd blacked out the lesson of the shower) on being so noticeably young in spirit we'd been included in this gathering of our juniors. I suppose I will die with the still-fresh remembrance of Shel's struggle for composure when our young hostess greeted us as naked as the collection of children frolicking round her comely bottom. The only time I've seen my decorous husband so determined at facial control was at a dinner where he was seated next to a jolly, motherly-looking lady with a bristling, Jerry Colonna walrus mustache (its luxuriance not to be confused with standard superfluous hair). He knew he mustn't look, but his eyeballs wouldn't listen; above all, he felt he must fight his urge to *tell* the lady what had invaded her upper lip and to recite ancient Burma Shave roadside jingles. And at the summer lawn fete where the hostess greeted him in radiant nakedness (a fact not one guest ever remarked upon, then or later), though he admired the weather as well as the chick-pea dip and addressed himself with great seriousness to this nation's foreign policy, I knew with what vein-popping restraint he was choking back, "Excuse me, young lady, but YOU DON'T HAVE ANY CLOTHES ON!"

Another middle-aged couple we know were chatting amiably at a party of younger couples when—at some mysterious signal—everyone shucked their clothes and leaped into the host's pool. The woman elected to sit it out poolside and think lofty thoughts, not easy for her when she saw her fifty-three-year-old husband throw caution, clothes, and everything except his Fruit of the Looms to the suburban wind and join the young swimmers, an "I do this all the time" look of nonchalance on his face, and his boxer shorts ballooning with water like some strange striped-cotton life preserver.

Neither that couple, nor my playwright friend the goat lady, nor Shel and I are closed to change and innovation; we simply need our glasses sometimes for the fine points. I like to think I'm as eager to learn about new things as I was in my Girl Scout days. I've even been known to experiment. Which is how it happened a few years ago that I (onetime wearer of boned, long-line Merry Widows) ventured into the world bravely braless. I'd recklessly bought a backless gown for some event, and there was no hiding place beneath it for underwear. A friend took an oath on her husband's life that I looked okay, however, and the halter straps that tied around my neck seemed to give just the proper little hoist I hoped might let me get away with it.

Yet while I think most young women look lovely with their nice protuberances perking through soft fabrics, I wasn't so addled as to think it was the right look for *me,* and that's where I drew the line. Or rather, drew on the adhesive bandage strips. The idea came from the saleswoman who sold me the gown, after I told her that though I loved it, I was worried I might embarrass myself if I got chilly when I wore it. Just stick the little one-inch strips on, she advised; *lots* of her customers did that and found there was no need to worry about pop-ups.

It worked! I felt comfortable, dashingly contemporary, moderately alluring—yet not aggressive. But though I may have pulled that off, retribution came in a different sort of pull-off. The little adhesive strips, this consumer can report, had never been nipple-tested when they were promoted as "ouchless." Many people claim that my screams were heard in Detroit, and the person who shares my life—that sunshine husband—locked himself into the bathroom and cowered there till the all-clear.

If the Girl Scouts of America hadn't failed me when I turned to them, I might have worked out some of this stuff on a reasonable schedule. It's also possible I wouldn't have accepted quite so many article assignments (and asked all those nosy questions) concerning sexual attitudes among women of all ages had I not been curious still about what other people are really doing. Or maybe things would have been different if the age of sensual enlightenment had been courteous enough to dawn a little earlier. But the truth is, it probably wouldn't have changed things at all, even if I *had* been born in time for the Sexual Revolution. My parents wouldn't have let me go to it anyway. Not, at least, if it were being held in the summer; I was never allowed to go *anywhere* in polio season. And in the winter, they made me wear leggings.

Late Entry

"What do you do?" says the dinner partner on my left. He's asking the man on my right, though, not me. Then he asks it again, this time skipping the woman beginning her gazpacho on his other side. She and I have bright fixed smiles; in another second my gums will probably bleed. The other nonperson is also in her forties, and I can tell this has happened to her (it turns out she's a designer) as often as to me. But *this* time I hear my voice break through the masculine exchange of job data. "Glad you asked," I shrill. "I'm a topless nuclear physicist."

Perhaps because I'm what's classified as "late bloomer," my—as they say—flowering is still so tentative that I'm thorny, impossible to please. Ignore me, like that dinner partner, and I'll bristle at what I see as an implicit assumption that a cute little old middle-aged blonde like me spends her days bouncing through Bonwit's. But *ask* me, "What do you do?"

and I'll probably resent, just as strenuously as my unemployed friends, the insinuation that you have to be salaried to be "interesting." My nominee for the Awesome Mental Health Award is the fortyish woman who, I'm told, boomed at a cocktail party, "What do I do about *what?*"

Even middle-aged women who have been working for years report variations on the same problem. One I know happens to be a tenured professor, but when the stranger next to her at a dinner party sized her up, his idea of an appropriate conversational opener was: "It's nice to meet you; what does your husband do?" What a pity the seniors in her advanced philosophical logic class weren't there to admire the scholarly authority behind her raised middle finger.

It's not just the nervous grip on a career that can cause the random vulgar gesture or, at the least, ambivalence in a woman of my vintage. Mine, after all, is the generation that has been besieged by rule changes, carpet-bombed for twenty-five years by contradictory messages. When our children were growing up, we were told that if we didn't *have* to work, our place was home raising them. That was the consensus of the "experts," few of whom troubled over such frivolities as inclination, temperament, training, to say nothing of what contributions we might have made to a society that saw us as a Monolith of Moms. If, as I did, you took all the fifties good mothering advice too seriously, you could get the impression that a child deprived of its mother's full-time focus might climb towers twenty years later and start shooting up the citizenry. The headlines would say, MOTHER CHOSE WORK, KID GOES BERSERK; the story would give your name, address, and alphabetize your inadequacies.

Doctrine started changing about ten years ago when studies done at universities and hospitals around the country began indicating that children who are well cared for by outsiders fare just as well as those with stay-home mothers, that kids turn out best when mothers work or don't work according to a woman's own sense of herself. Not that the all-time final pronouncement is in, but it's hard cheese for those of us who went by the book when books had the opposite hypothesis. Well, okay, things change, Dr. Spock was sound on a lot of things, he's updated himself, and I'd forgive him if he hadn't revised his life, too, by taking a bride who's so much younger than both he *and* I. (In the last year or so, there's been a resurgence of stay-home-if-you-don't-have-to-work counsel to young mothers. Did *our* kids turn out so well on the same advice that it's time to resurrect and dump it indiscriminately on a whole new generation of mothers?)

What's hard to take, now that we have ripened by several decades, is being told today by so many of the experts that—for our mental well-being—we *ought* to be employed. A lot of us would like to be, but those experts aren't so quick to provide updated data telling middle-aged women how—if we took the old stay-home edicts as gospel—we might come up with job experience for this toughest of labor markets. And it must be just as galling not to want or need to work and feel you ought to apologize.

Self-realization is a nicety, of course, compared to such pressures as survival. Generations of poor, particularly minority, women didn't have the comparative luxury of waiting for experts to tell them what's good for the family that happens to be hungry. But for an emerging group of middle-class women, survival has become an issue in the past few years, too. Yesterday's generous insurance policy and well-rounded nest egg don't go far toward supporting today's widow or the wife of an ill or unemployed husband (perhaps the very guy whose favorite long-playing record used to be, "No wife of *mine* is ever going to work!").

And there's also another new class of the instant and unaccustomed poor. My friend Maggie qualified for membership in it, like so many other women our age, when her quarter century husband came down to breakfast one morning and asked to have his eggs over easy and his marriage over, period. In that same Early American breakfast nook, Maggie had been telling him for years that she'd like to prepare for a profession, and his answer was as unvarying as his egg order: "Homemaking is the noblest profession of them all!" The trouble with the "noblest profession" was that at compulsory retirement time, it had neither health plan nor retirement benefits to reward twenty-five years of service. Maggie didn't get so much as a gold watch, and although she was awarded their home as settlement, like many women with no job, poor prospects, nothing even to parlay into a lie on a résumé, and an ex-husband with both a modest income and nubile new bride, Maggie's borrowing over her head now to make mortgage payments.

As that little group of my bolting friends I described earlier has proved, it isn't just middle-aged husbands who are asking out; seasoned wives are initiating the late-life split, too. They do it far less frequently, but the numbers are unprecedented, and most forecasts threaten that divorce figures will get worse—no matter which sex beats it out the door first. And whatever the reasons behind the statistics—no fault, clear fault, or double fault—an army of women who never needed money before and has never worked (at least not in decades) is part of the numerical fallout.

The last time *I* made employment agency rounds was in the early fifties. I was twenty, then—a just-married art major dropout given to informing personnel directors, "I want to do something cre-A-tive!" They rolled their eyeballs, and I took a sales job at Lord & Taylor, where it was soon clear that management had tabbed me for big things. Why else, I asked myself, would they have notified our department that in the event of nuclear attack, I had been chosen to guard the Young People's Accessories' cash register? Well, no wonder; I *did* stand out. It was the year that Anne Fogarty horsehair crinolines were fashion de rigueur—particularly for an upwardly mobile saleswoman—and I wore several at a time in shellacked tiers that made me look like a walking Tiffany shade. Maybe they figured all I had to do to nuclear-proof a cash register was sit on it, like a demented little tea cozy. Despite the honor, however, no missiles fell on Young People's Accessories that season, so I moved on to doing my best to impart lyricism to Montgomery Ward catalog copy. But art would have to wait. I perceived a higher calling and traded in my crinolines for a maternity wardrobe, just as all my friends were doing. It was time, we said, to get ready for motherhood.

Nobody forced me into that timetable, of course; there were women—even in those narrowly prescribed days—who were independent enough not to see life as an immutable schedule. Yet most of us played it pretty close to that well-ordered fifties routine, and today we're called empty nesters. A lot of us love it. The vacated nest can hatch new beginnings—an opportunity for untried or favorite causes, creativity, school, delicious solitude. For some, it means time for the tennis court and the happy courting of old husbands—one's own and, in some cases, other people's.

Many mothers have scandalized themselves by adjusting so well to late-learned autonomy that the most beloved of children, home too long on a visit, can send them wistfully, secretly, checking departure schedules. The message isn't always clear, and how we feel can depend on what day you ask.

Example of ambivalence: Claudia, at twenty-one, comes "home" for dinner on a night so cold our car engine freezes and we can't return her to her apartment later—or find a cab. For months I'd been fantasizing that she'd come back and live with us before she graduated, maybe for a year or two; she's such good company, and—after all—we get on so well. So, to demonstrate the comforts of living in our bosom, I bring my daughter a cup of hot chocolate after she's tucked in bed that night. Because I'll stop at nothing, there's even a marshmallow floating on top (a little stale; it's a Thanksgiving leftover), and she is pleased, puzzled, and too polite to point out that in all the years she and her brother were full-time residents I never once made hot chocolate.

When I slip back into bed, Shel asks where I've been and, also puzzled, but less tactful than his daughter was, asks, "Did she *want* hot chocolate?" and then, "Well, I don't understand why you didn't ask her first." I explain about surprises. I make a speech about spontaneity and how offerings, when expected, lose their inherent delight. He doesn't understand, we exchange credos well past midnight, and it ends with a gush of resentment (it used to be my teary Old Faithful) that hasn't erupted from me in over twenty years: "And *you* never bring me flowers when it isn't an *occasion!*" (But we're older now, so we laugh and go to sleep.)

In the early morning—a space I have come to cherish as quiet coffee and newspaper time before I settle in at my desk—I get a stomachache because this grown woman who is my daughter goes off without breakfast. Another few days of togetherness and my talent for regression would be so out of hand that I'd be lying awake nights waiting for her key in the door, and in no time I'd have her wrapped up in an emotional receiving blanket. Ah, yes, she is the darling of my heart; she likes me, too, and can even say so. But we are two grown, stubborn women, and we have to do our loving in separate quarters now that it has become our daily habit.

In one of her stories, Tillie Olsen wrote about a woman's "reconciled peace" in the solitude that comes when one is no longer "forced to move to the rhythm of other people." However pleasing or jarring old rhythms may have been, the challenge comes in finding new and natural ones. Most of the women I know have found the empty nest, after a little emotional redecorating, feels comfortable again. Nevertheless, there are alarming empty nest studies indicating that when our birds go off, some of us go off our birds; habit and the customs of a culture and a lifetime leave us picking through the straw, wondering what to do with the rest of our lives. And it's because depression (along with drug and alcohol problems) afflicts us so-called empty nest mothers with particular frequency and viciousness that we are often counseled that work is an antidote, even a life preserver. Work can, it's true, help people get some leverage on depression; the emotional need to work can be nearly as clamorous as the economic need (many of us have been graced by both pressures). But depression itself is so immobilizing that a woman with little or no experience is facing the rigors of the job hunt and its built-in ego devastators when she is least equipped emotionally to take them on. Just reading the help wanted ads for a couple of days is enough to give you a pain in the classifieds; what's available for most of us seems less likely to counter depression than to confer it.

A college acquaintance quit law school to get married twenty-three years ago when she came down with a case of premature pregnancy, the first of four children. She and her husband agreed that her "place was at home." That is, until he decided their place was in divorce court; she didn't agree to *that,* but it was final and no fault two years ago. I don't know their financial arrangements, but last time I glimpsed her, she was setting out lemon Jell-Os from the service side of a cafeteria, looking as acerb as her wares.

I told a psychiatrist I know about this woman, and she said, "Your college pal must be a masochist; some women take jobs like that to show everybody what bastards their ex-husbands are." Yet one doesn't have to be a card-carrying, Jell-O–pushing masochist to discover that the deadly job may be all that's available if you're long out of work and short on credentials. And the interesting job, on the other hand, may offer starvation wages. Another woman I know ("Most Promising, Class of '51") was recently offered fifty dollars a week to do a full-time editorial job for which—by talent and education—she is eminently qualified. "Listen," said the young woman making the munificent offer on behalf of a small local magazine, "I can get any number of other suburban housewives who haven't worked in twenty years to do it free." The awful thing is that despite the minimum wage law, she probably can; at least my friend had the dignity to say, "Well, you can't get *me,* tootsie!" The story would be a lot better if the capper were an inspiring "Today she has her dream job!" The capper, in fact, is a crusher; she doesn't have any. Like my friend the widow, who also hasn't worked in twenty years, she's had other offers, but none was for employment.

In the past few years, some state legislatures have begun addressing themselves to the problems of older women (particularly those widowed, divorced, or deserted) who need to find work, and women's groups, colleges, and universities are designing programs and workshops for the late-entry careerist. It's a beginning, it's encouraging, but need outpaces remedial measures every day.

Self-image can be the worst problem of all: egos in need of resuscitation, if not intensive care. If some of us were directors of personnel, we'd be the first to stamp ARE YOU KIDDING? on our own job applications. I once did an article about a state Department of Mental Health program that had a remarkable success record in developing new ways to help the hard-core long-term unemployed to find work. And what impressed me most during the interviews were the things I was told about women very much like me. "We've been extremely successful in placing men who haven't worked for years," a program psychologist said, "recovered alcoholics, former psychiatric patients—you name the problem. But the people with the least self-confidence are women who have been longtime homemakers; they simply don't think of what they've done as having any value."

Another counselor who helped run the program said, "Most of the middle-aged women we work with are so accustomed to someone running interference for them that even looking for a job is a terrifying prospect. They think their only possibility for getting one is through somebody they know; they want it served up." I'm all sympathy. For years, I longed to hear a knock at my door, followed by a tender voice announcing, "Hello, my darling . . . I'm your job!"

So it's encouraging, considering the rigors of late entry, that a number of women *have* managed a delayed launching into work that is exciting to them, sustaining, intellectually rewarding (though rarely financially so), some say life-giving. Many of them say it took heart-pounding bravado or just plain faking until they learned a couple of trade tricks and some vocabulary. But given a chance to stick around till you get a grip on the patois, who can't learn to say "point of sale" or "cost-effective analysis" or "show me the bottom line!"? Getting one's middle-aged metatarsus in the door is, of course, the tricky part, but I know women who delayed careers till their offspring were grown—or nearly so—and managed to make the late entry. And to see some of them in action today, you'd think they were born holding briefcases.

My friend Sherry's a briefcase holder in point. At fifty, she's a TV producer who, with no experience in broadcasting, got her first full-time job in twenty years when her first husband died ten years ago and has worked her way up to executive producer and take-home pay few working women can match. "It's a whole new life," she says, "but the tough part—and it still gives me trouble—has been coming into business from a wife-mother-community orientation and setting different expectations for myself. If I'd started younger, I'd have picked up more technical skills. I've never faked it, like a lot of men do, though I'd be further along if I had. But women who start late have one real advantage over those whose total experience has been in the career world. We've developed more *human* skills, cultivated certain sensibilities that make others really touch base with us. Colleges recruit foreign students so American kids can benefit from other experiences, and in the world of business, *we're* the ones who bring something valuable from another culture."

Gloria is another old friend who hadn't worked since her first pregnancy made her quit an NBC research job in 1958. Six years ago, in her forties, she began as part-time staffer for a Connecticut weekly. "I was so grateful," she says, "and so dumb that I sometimes worked for nothing because the paper was struggling then, and when I got fifty dollars a week—me, housewife, mother of three persons—I couldn't figure out why anyone would pay me to be so happy." She scrambled up the staff to feature editor, columnist, arts reviewer, editorial writer; then went on to be assistant managing editor of a New England daily.

Gloria used to live in a house that *The New York Times* described in an article as "one of Fairfield County's showplaces." She had a tennis court, a swimming pool, and threw dinner parties so elegant that "having her back" gave tremors to the insecure (me, for instance). She also had a high-powered husband who made all the above possible. "I used to feel I was living in another woman's skin, and guilty not to love all those luxuries," she says. "But the small house I live in now feels right to me, and my job didn't kill my marriage; it simply allowed me to see that it had died and that working is as natural and intrinsic to me as breathing. I'm just another one of those women of my generation who never questioned the idea that you had to earn the right to a career by raising children and giving flawless dinner parties first."

Most people, I suppose, could find enough solace in their very own tennis court and swimming pool to compensate for the career that never blossomed. Or, having renounced all that, they'd find themselves forced to settle for a lot less than Brenda Starr–dom. But then Gloria, even with her own court, played such terminal tennis, her backhand was probably a divine signal she was meant for another form of human expression. And though we live in an era where lip service has it that to work or not to work has equal prestige, if the woman who "does something" didn't have a generally higher (if secret) status, what motivates the Bouvier sisters and the Mses. Vanderbilt and Ford and so many of the less-affluent but unneedy rest of us?

The long-range view is as cloudy with complexities, and has some of the same moral dilemmas and implications, as the Bakke case. As the economy tightens along with available jobs, as mandatory retirement ends and unemployment worsens among minorities and teens, as Ph.D.'s take factory jobs, what *is* rightful stalking ground for the late-entry middle-aged woman? Will we find ourselves competing with our own kids for openings that get scarcer each year? Many middle-aged women work out of the same economic need that most men do, and ought to have the same opportunities. But for those of us whose work is impelled by needs that, though deep, are less than our present survival, how egalitarian can a society be to accommodate even us? Well, given the odds against our finding work, I think what we can grab onto and handle is rightfully, ethically ours. A great many of us deferred this aspect of ourselves for most of our lives, and if we can beat the jobs out of the bushes now, who has the moral authority to instruct us that it's our duty to stand aside, or sit home, again? And if we are widowed, divorced, or deserted in the future, will it be easier to find work even later in our lives?

It's too bad, though, that volunteerism and the worthy causes supported by it may be fashion's latest casualty. If a woman engages her skills in self-satisfying ways by contributing them, why should she be pressured to do something less useful or stimulating (maybe even stultifying) because a salary endorses it as "real"? And though growing numbers of our daughters are quite properly refusing to be relegated into career choices by their genitals, many of *us* are just now preparing to enter some of those increasingly suspect fields. Schools of nursing, for instance, have been reporting record enrollments of older women, and why not? There's no reason for a late-starting careerist to shun work that attracts her and for which she may have the true vocation just because, traditionally, it *has* been women's province.

As for my own delayed entry, I don't know the psychic reasons for that advanced case of foot-dragging. Like most of reading America, I've seen a number of articles about the fear-of-success syndrome from which women of all ages—not only my "home is best" generation—are said to suffer. I've read the studies done by Radcliffe's president, psychologist Matina Horner, showing that many women equate career success with social rejection, loss of femininity, damage to society's very balance, and I've noted that fear-of-success courses are appearing on curricula all over the country. *My* career evasions had always struck me as fear of trying, fear of failure, rather than of success, but the studies explain that those are simply different faces of the same reluctance. Of course, there's a good chance that my problem has been nothing more interesting than spectacular laziness, and I probably should either admit it (and stop trying to find respectable diagnoses) or sign up for one of those fear-of-success classes. But if I took a course like that, I guess I'd have to tell the teacher about my mother-the-Hungarian, who—when I was a teen—greeted my return from every social occasion with the Four Questions: "Were you popular?" "Are you considered witty?" "Did they like your dress?" and the *real* biggie, "Did anyone ask you to dance?"

Nearly three decades later, things hadn't changed much because I'd been writing for a year or so when I told her that my first cover story for *The New York Times Magazine,* a parody in *New York,* articles in *Harper's, Playboy,* and some Chicago publications would all appear within the week and she said, "That's nice, dear, but what *else?*"

Maybe there's a clue in such things to why it took me so many years to risk rejection slips, maybe a tiny hint of where the fear-of-success factor comes into it. Suppose (as wild hypothesis) I *had* succeeded, beyond probability, fantasy, and all the way to Pulitzerhood. I mean, what could I have told my mother if *none of the judges asked me to dance*?

As I look back, it's clear that I could have stayed home with my children and scribbled away; certainly there was nothing to stop me once they started school. I made stirring resolutions, instead, like the one on my twenty-eighth birthday giving myself two more years to alter the course of my life. (That meant begin writing.) And from the moment I commit-

ted myself to that resolve—stand back for the inspiring part—
it took me only fourteen more years to run out and buy typing
paper.

Meanwhile, I'd turned forty-two when Paul went off to
Krishna and Claudia to college, and there I was, a brooding
plucked hen in the classic empty nest. Except, that summer of
'73, I had company—people who had done at least as badly as I
had: Haldeman and Mitchell, Dean and Ulasewicz. I don't
know why that daily procession of characters on television
struck me as Chaucerian, but when I finally attacked the
virgin tablet, the result was the long footnoted poem about the
hearings called "The Waterbury Tales." I worried a bit that
the verse that began: "The Ehrlichman explan the word
'coverte' / He look lyk he eat babys for desserte" was a shade
cruel, then laughed at myself; who'd ever read the thing?

A few people did. *The New Republic* bought and printed
it; the next week Reuters dispatched it to newspapers around
the world: *Time* ran it as its lead, *Newsweek* nearly as promi-
nently. There was a Krakatoa of mail—book nibbles from
publishing houses, interview invitations for radio and TV, job
offers, including one from a newspaper syndicate to do a daily
feature for the next five years. It was a nice way to start, particularly since I'd have been pleased with a by-line in *Dry Cleaning World*. And now that everybody I knew had heard about
my new career—thank God, I could quit! But editors from
daunting publications called and said, "Let's have a look at
the rest of your work ... send whatever's in the trunk."
Whatever's in the trunk? How could they publish mothballs?

My nervous system shifted into emotional overdrive. I
couldn't sleep or digest; I'd forgotten the techniques for such
niceties. Dazed, crazed, and mumbling, I'd career around the
house granting imaginary interviews. Shel would hear me
muttering in our bedroom, and he'd burst in, hollering, "Who

the hell are you always talking to in here?" I was chatting with Chekhov, of course; I was giving literary critics *my* opinions.

I began to identify with "the pig woman." She was a witness at the famous Hall-Mills murder trial in the twenties, and her testimony was crucial to the outcome because she'd been known to wander around the spot in lovers' lane where the corpse had been found. But the poor cracked old pig woman was ailing, and to get her statement they had to carry her into the courtroom in her bed. I'd seen photographs of her, head raised an inch off her pillow, judge leaning forward to hear her gasps of testimony. And I knew that if I ever mustered the nerve to go on one of those television talk shows that had begun calling, I'd have to be carried in on my bed, just like the lady of the swine.

But as Dr. Faustus discovered, when the devil gets you in middle age, he's got you by the varicosities. "You want a career now?" *my* devil whispered. "You want a by-line, baby, that someday at least twenty-seven people in America will recognize instantly?"

"Yes, Devil, yes." I cried. "Roast me with early hot flashes! Dent me with cellulite! Let my dog succumb to premature flatulence." (That's the one the devil, that gonif, picked first.)

But success sniffed late can be just as vexing a social problem. Talk it up, and (old convictions die hard) you may be punished. What if your pals think you're bragging and desert you? What if the gods make you fall on your nose just to keep in touch with gravity? On the other hand, the *need* to tell pops out like chicken pox. Search the world, there isn't a more modest and reticent woman than my friend the late-blooming playwright, yet even she was so radioactive with joy the week before her first play was staged that she couldn't resist telling a department store saleswoman, "I'm looking for a coat that I can wear to the *first performance of my play* next week."

The clerk, perhaps in sisterhood, perhaps in pursuit of commerce, leaped to the challenge. "Here's just the coat!" she cried. "You can play it *up*—or *down*. *This* way" (collar up) "for evening performances. *This* way" (collar down) "for matinees. Don't you think?" Both agreed—lost in joy of their respective crafts—that a hint of turtleneck underneath lent the proper casual look for "your basic rehearsal." Well, after all, we have to wear *something* until we can wrap ourselves in whatever becomes a legend most.

For me, the strangest part of getting that first bit of literary exposure was that after a life's inability, refusal, fright, or whatever it was that came between me and getting down to it, writing became the only human activity I *could* manage. And now I'm so dependent on daily work that I sometimes awaken in a sweat of terror because I hear the great all-powerful THEY out there saying, "It's all been a mistake, faker; turn in your Smith-Corona!"

This emotional dependency seems characteristic of the late bloomer. Judith Guest, who wrote her first book, the bestselling *Ordinary People,* in her forties, said during an interview, "Writing is my survival," but the feeling isn't limited to authors. My friends who now are immersed in work they spent most of their lives not doing are astounded by the zeal, even passion, they put into it. "For me, it's sanity," says the one who at fifty is a fledgling lobbyist. "It's the only thing I've ever had that's all *mine,"* says the catering consultant (reminding me of my widowed friend's "The best thing about a job is you don't have to wait for *it* to telephone"). These are long-married women who, by their own evaluations, have sturdy unions. Sometimes the challenge hasn't been learning new tricks, but juggling them within old marriages.

Indoctrination, if not habit, makes us placate our guilt gods variously. Some assume a superdomesticity as if to prove work isn't making them renege on old unspoken contracts. One woman turns her entire fat paycheck over to her husband so he can dole out her "allowance" just as he had done for the past twenty-two years that she didn't work. Another gray-streaked meteorite forfeited her latest salary increase. "I'd have been earning more than Leonard, and he'd drive me crazy to quit."

Jessie, who is forty-two and mother of three, says that marrying her well-known husband-the-musician was "as close as I ever expected to get to achievement." Her own deferred achievement dazes but delights her since the public relations business she started in New York a few years ago began attracting a full roster of clients. "My husband loves the fact that I'm making money now," she says, "and hates that I've stopped making soup. But I'm getting over the guilt about giving him less motherly care and attention now that I've discovered I can afford to invite him out to lunch instead." (One new worker's guilt vanished the day her husband stared into their refrigerator and wailed, "Nobody washed the *fruit!*")

A woman in her fifties told me that what pleases her most about working is packing her own suitcase when she's on the road, a duty first her father's "pleasure," then her husband's. Other women with whom I've spoken say that freeing themselves from lifelong dependencies was as rewarding as newly discovered job competence and nearly as liberating as the invention of panty hose. I know what they mean. Though I'm now reasonably confident that I will sell the products of my typewriter, what sends me into paroxysms of self-approval are things most people can do without second thoughts: renting cars when I'm on assignment; following road maps without having to stand on my head to face the direction I'm going; making friends in transit; being alone in the middle of the world. Yet one snowy evening recently I went to a meeting of "career achievers" of my sex, and when the woman who had picked me up parked several slushy blocks from where we were going, I found myself thinking petulantly, *Shel* would have dropped me at the door in this weather. And another time, after I'd spent an exhilarating work month traveling (and equal time congratulating myself for it), I woke up in a Des Moines Holiday Inn with my aging thumb in my mouth and knew that you can only liberate some of the people some of the time.

Maybe I'd better back up a bit here. That "thumb-sucking" I was trying to be funny about was far from amusing at the time. What really took place was an attack of fear of something I couldn't name, yet so severe it nearly paralyzed me for two days and nights. I never slept during that time, and though I usually insist on room-darkening shades *and* closed draperies, I wouldn't even turn off the lights. When I called Shel and tried to manipulate him into "ordering" me to come home, he was too smart to do it. I had just enough control left not to ask any stranger I could find into my room to hold my hand through the night—but I considered it. Karen DeCrow, in a letter to *The New York Times* about an article it had run that defined agoraphobia as "incapacitating anxiety on traveling away from the safety of the home," said, "In a culture which has consistently doled out punishment to women who travel away from home (from unequal pay in the marketplace to blame for children who turn to drugs), it is no surprise that certain women, sensing the existential irony of their situation, actually refuse to leave home."

When Paul was eleven and Claudia was nine, I *did* take an outside job for more than a year. I asked them before I accepted it how they felt about having a working mother. Claudia said she didn't know, she'd never had one; Paul said he'd like to see some sample menus of what our meals would be like—both answers persuaded me that they were both ready to handle it. I wasn't. When the job required travel, I developed such a fear of airplanes my head trembled from takeoff to landing. I eventually got to see a copy of the psychological evaluation an executive-testing firm had made about my qualifications for the job before it was offered to me. My "strengths" listing was long, impressive, and probably inaccurate; my "weaknesses" contained only one sentence: "Her tests reveal great conflicts about taking time away from her wife / mother role, and she may never resolve them." It turned out that those tests had my number; I didn't resolve the conflicts, and when I quit and resumed my old persona, my head stopped shaking in airplanes. It's probably a good thing, too; if Paul's problems had begun in earnest during that brief time I worked, I'd never have let myself off the hook for what I did or didn't do.

So I don't have any idea whether that virulent anxiety attack in the Des Moines motel two years ago was some last-ditch invasion of my old ambivalence (I didn't even *have* any children living at home at the time), or some hormonal malfunction, or just an allergy to Iowa. I've worked around the country a number of times since, and it has never happened again, though I've kept an uneasy respect for the power of even a hit-and-run assault of whatever it was. (My worst regression since was the time in Colorado when I had dinner with a man I was interviewing and brought along the virgin tube of toothpaste I hadn't been able to pry open in my motel room. A kindly man, he uncapped it over pêche Melba without snickering.)

It's more than likely that if Shel had come to get me or ordered me home from Iowa as I tried to maneuver him into doing, I would have spent the rest of our lives telling him he'd interfered in my new career. And if what sent me climbing

191

those stucco motel walls was the last gasp of that voice in my head that asks, "Who said you're allowed to do this?" I'm aware that the bigmouthed interior voice has always been my very own. Shel has never said one career-discouraging word.

I suppose that a husband whose self-image hangs on being the sole or superior wage earner and having a loftier job title is, at best, a shaky partner. Whether such fragile egos can only go the marriage distance if old power bases remain unchallenged is anybody's guess. There just isn't much hard data, yet, on late-bloomery, its effects on long-established patterns and marital longevity. Perhaps many older women start to work *because* their marriages are strained, as a hedge against the breakup they know is coming. And sometimes the most hard-nosed "no wife of mine is ever going to work" husband begins to relax and enjoy as he feels the compensatory balm of a second and unaccustomed paycheck.

Shel has handled my new career from the start with a lot more equanimity than I have, yet even he gets shaken now and then. For over two decades, we lived as if I were in training for the Lestoil Olympics, and now I only do enough to ward off the Black Death (and only if he can prove there's a certified case on our block). He says that he sometimes feels he's living with Oscar in *The Odd Couple*. But last New Year's, in a hiccup of vestigial guilt, I volunteered to let him write my resolution. "What do you *really* want from me in the next year?" I asked.

"Subservience," he said. "Obedience and deference. But since I'm not going to get any of those from you, would you mind occasionally closing a drawer?"

Once, when I was shouting hold-the-fort orders at him while I was getting ready to go on the road, he hollered after me, "Hey, sir . . . your purse is open!" Otherwise, he's weathering the career and his hunger pangs nicely, though people tend to sidle up to him at parties with a conspiratorial "What's it *really* like now, with Judy working all the time?" There's often a sort of undertone that the way I'm spending my days lately must be as hard on domestic relations as if I'd taken to peddling perversions in the Loop at high noon.

A man I know who encouraged his wife to go back to work now that their children are grown says that he finds his wife infinitely more attractive sexually than he has in years. "She's so full of life and enthusiasm," he says, "and there's such an air of assurance about her since she's getting to be a hotshot in the real estate world that it's really quite a turn-on for me. And *that's* the problem! After our kids left home, but before she started working, I used to look forward to our weekends together, because I was too tired for sex during the week. But the weekends are her busiest time now for showing properties, and she'll say, 'Sure, I'd love to come home early and make love on the floor, dear, but I have appointments all day.' It's very confusing!"

"When a late bloomer's husband feels threatened," says sociologist Dr. William Simon (a onetime Kinsey associate), "it usually isn't sexual fear, even though—whether she responds to them or not—other men may indeed be flashing sexual signals to his wife. If her sense of competence is being affirmed by her job, life has suddenly become more colorful and varied, and what could be more aphrodisiacal? But what her husband probably dreads most is losing his lifelong monopoly on reporting the world to her." Simon, however, was quick to admit that since there is very little data on so-called late bloom and late entry, he—like I—was only speculating. (Besides, he said the late bloomer "often has an air of sophistication, of someone who has redesigned herself into something more, or better, or different, and it gives her an advantage over younger women and makes her very attractive to men"—so clearly the man is a brilliant thinker.)

Dr. Simon, like other sociologists and the psychiatrists, psychologists, and counselors I questioned, solidly endorses the middle-aged woman's right to work, whether emotional or economic need impels her. But most of the professionals counsel us to take a cold-eyed look at the risks. Some caution that the good old affliction, identity crisis, can come from breaking one's sense of connection with the past; they warn that the two most incompatible human desires are the wish for new experience and the wish for security. They also point to the perils of new vulnerability—exposure to rejection, failure, and what Simon calls "the disillusion of finding out what most men discovered long ago: how crappy that glamorous world of work really is." Which is doubtlessly true; many women of my age are indeed strangers, and perhaps naïve ones, to the work terrain. Still, most of the experts haven't spent much time within the prescribed borders of *our* lives (and their track record hasn't been all that good with us anyway), so I suspect there's a lot to learn for both front-liners *and* theorists. But given the shocks of the last few decades, to have made it into one's middle years should have been risk-taking practice enough to inure anybody. Furthermore, most of us are familiar with the adage "If at first you don't succeed, you'll be used to it later on."

Not long ago, a sweet-faced sixty-three-year-old woman (forty-two years a wife, mother of four) applied for her first Social Security card. "Do you mean you've never worked before in your whole life?" said the incredulous young clerk. "The hell I didn't!" she exploded. "I just never got *paid* for it." She is obviously attempting her job debut later than most, and even if she's lucky enough to find work she likes, she probably has some bad times ahead. It happens to most late bloomers, those days of despairing that we'll never "catch up." I know all about such days, when the putting together of just one re-spectable sentence thumbs its prose at me, and I rage, rage against the dying of the brain cells. What, I scream at myself, have you been *doing* all these years?

"Ah, well," says the temporizer within (an indulgent and *much* too practiced voice), "better late . . ."

Sum of These Days

Better late is one thing; a Valentine's Day party not yet given by springtime quite another. What happened was, I was working on this book, and I got so absorbed in writing about the nervous romantic tic that makes me give the dopey party every year, I forgot to twitch. That sort of thing happens a lot lately; I put something down on paper and think I've disposed of any further obligation toward it. For instance, I used to go to a calisthenics class regularly, but after I described the exertions in an article, I got the idea somehow that exercise and I were settled, that I'd taken care of it in perpetuity. Well, it doesn't work that way, and I have the thighs to prove it.

On the other hand, this absorption in the thing I do, though at least half of the time it scares, isolates, disappoints, and depresses me, is the most welcome present my birthdays ever brought me. Not that my special brand of absentminded forgetting-to-send-invitations (and falling-down-escalators) distraction is a cure for whatever midlife crises might be waiting to try a person on for size. Yet if I came to any conclusion after the last few years' worth of conversations and interviews with women, it's (hardly surprising) that those who were withstanding life's trick shots best were really involved, *immersed,* in what they did every day.

Whatever it was that engaged them didn't necessarily have a job classification or take-home pay, though I'd be the last to minimize either and the first to complain about how difficult these things are to come by for the long-unemployed. And as I've already said of our mothers' generation, the older women who seemed zestiest (given reasonably cooperative health) were those who stayed interested in a world larger than self and inevitable changes in appearance. So having worked that out, wouldn't you think that when I read a report claiming sardine consumption counteracts wrinkles, I could have curbed myself from cornering the King Oscar catch before that very nightfall? Perhaps it was only a form of propitiating at every altar, of hedging all bets, like my friend who not only jogs every day, but does it to, around, and back from a local nursing home as reminder of where he might go if he lets up.

There never has been such a ripe time for books and articles telling us "how to." There are almost more advisers than problems to go around, but never mind; if you don't care for one guru's guidelines, a profusion of other authorities awaits with lists, charts, and life-reversing counsel of their own for the imperfect reader. We can choose experts who invent problems to complement theories (like Johnny Carson's Karnak who supplies questions for answers), or experts whose specialty is challenging the theories that have been lying around for a year or two without astonishing anyone anymore, or—

even better—sages who make up new words. Best yet, we can obliterate things we don't like by digging up an authority with the right set of negating statistics. One survey of what turned out to be fewer than forty women showed that premenstrual depression hardly exists. Another document virtually ruled out menopausal hot flashes, and I do wish my friends (many of whom were put on estrogen to keep them "forever young" until they learned it could make them sooner dead) would remember that when they break out in their illusory sweats.

I once watched a documentary about penguins and learned that any penguin that moves with determination will be followed by the others, even into mass drowning. I have to admit that I've been a frozen-brained acquiescent penguin for most of my life and have toddled along after some very assertive birds. A few of them even changed direction with the season; I'm glad I was too old and tired to join the parade led by the couple who electrified America with that "open marriage" book. It must have been disorienting to their devotees when the authors' *next* literary divulgence was something they'd unearthed called sexual fidelity.

The main trouble with hot-off-the-press expertise is not that it often can be modishly silly or opportunistic, but that it can be very cruel. Real people with complicated problems are out there in the reading / viewing audience: The father whose fourteen-year-old daughter hanged herself after years of therapy reads the headlined story (it quotes six authorities with six theories) called "Why Kids Kill Themselves"; the autistic child's bewildered mother (no one knows yet what causes autism) sees a TV play that depicts the parents of autistic children as rejecting; the cancer patient learns she or he subconsciously "wanted" it. I know too many people who have shuffled themselves or their children from savior to self-announced savior and learned that if this year's miracle therapy makes one's nose drop off in five years, being an "expert" means never having to say you're sorry

Not that there's anything inherently wrong with the struggle to organize, make coping strategies, attack what flesh is heir to in an orderly manner. Nor is there anything wrong in making mistakes on the way to progress; bless those willing to take the risks. It's just that we could use a lot more humility toward what *isn't* known about the afflictions of mind and body, respect for how much our lives may depend on bio-chemical and genetic mystery, chance, serendipity, and, above all, we could do with some shyness about yelling "Eureka!" I think if there's one discovery we've made over the years it's that (wherever they rank on the spectrum of intelligence and integrity) the keepers of our minds, bodies, journals, and tribal customs have as much trouble putting hospital corners on chaos as most of the rest of us.

Which doesn't mean we shouldn't keep looking for answers, or that *I'm* pleased to be so short of them. What with the vogue for certainty, it's embarrassing to read back over these chapters and find that though I've ventured some speculation and timid empiricism, one phrase that keeps asserting itself is a cowardly "I don't know." Like A. E. Housman, I often feel "a stranger and afraid / In a world I never made," and if I'd known a smoother route to middle age, I'd have taken it. But the good thing about not being an expert is that the nonauthority field is so uncrowded nobody bothers to kick you out of it for scratching your head a lot and mumbling.

Among the things I didn't find out much more about than I knew when I started was which of the old marriages I sniffed around would be bouncing along in another five years, and I wouldn't presume to sort out which ones ought to be. I *did* list some non sequiturs from the old marriage I know best, but who has the goods on the couple next door? Who can pick out the important snapshots from anybody else's family album or evaluate scientifically the import of what was said or not said in the emergency room when the kid was hurt (or maybe took an overdose), and what was said, or carefully not said, after discovered adultery or when the job was lost or after the surgery that changed one body and two lives. Scenes from a marriage can only be interpreted by the principal actors, and predicting long runs is very chancy enterprise.

And I'm no better at divorce appraisals. After a great deal of talking and interviewing, damned if I know which divorces that ended vintage unions signaled new life at long last or merely termination-by-trendiness. I witnessed breakups in some of the nicest places I visited (but then I didn't have to live or sleep there). I saw monogamous liaisons that made me think of stirring words like *commitment, character, loyalty, solidity,* but I *also* saw women put all their emotional eggs in one bastard and live to regret it—too often on the day they first heard about their barely pubescent replacements. And I didn't formulate any all-occasion rules about whether, in the middle of her life, a woman ought to know more about her sexuality than she's learned through domestic relations, or whether—mid pleasures and phalluses—there's no place like home.

As for maternal adjustment to the empty nest and feelings toward the children who once filled it, attitudes in my little sampling varied with how much life was left in that empty nest and the liveliness of the remaining occupants; I found no one-size-fits-all panaceas. Many women seem to have struck a midlife balance with their grown children that's worthy of being case-studied in a textbook on the healthy family. Others with whom I've spoken continue to live through their offspring as they did in years past, pronounce it "enough" and "satisfying," and who's to say that what shouldn't work never does? In middle age, some of the women I know made peace at last with themselves and the kids who disappointed or bewildered them; still others became distracted by radically changed work and / or love lives. And some of us have survived through hardening our hearts against the child we never could fathom. But as Margaret Drabble wrote of a mother who closed out a hostile daughter in *The Ice Age,* "A hardened heart is as painful as a soft one."

We have heard several decades worth of theories and countertheories about our children and how they got that way; I have no new ones. My friend Barbara, though, has invented what she swears is an immutable rule for predicting what sort of parent will spawn what variety of offspring. Barbara's theory is: "Straight makes crooked, crooked makes straight." You had only to watch the *I, Claudius* series on "Masterpiece Theatre" to see that Barbara's theory might have something to it; Germanicus and Agrippina were about the only straight shooters in their part of the Roman Empire, and *they* parented Caligula. "Straight makes crooked" would, indeed, explain why some of the pleasantest people have some of the most tiresome children, but what about those splendid folks we all know who produce flawless citizens? Well, if life held still for classifications, what would a yet-unborn generation of experts have to do once they get here?

The joys and alarums of grandparenting have been left out of this, probably because I don't have any firsthand knowledge of them, nor do most of my friends. I suppose that in itself is a sign of our middle-class, middle-aged times. Most of our parents were being called some variation on grandma and grandpa when they were as old as my friends and I are now, but *our* children are marrying later, if at all, and often choosing not to parent. Another contemporary development was reflected in an anonymous guest editorial in *The New York Times*, its writer a woman who had come to terms with her son's seven-year living-together arrangement, but was horrified that the couple chose not to marry when a child was expected. (My own mother could have handled that with confidence; she would have had my lover and me arrested and taken the grandchild home for *Dobos torte*.)

I suspect if I'm ever going to be anyone's granny, I'll be the sort whose "kitchee kitchee koos" will be followed shortly by "Take your kid home; Granny's got a deadline" (even when Granny doesn't). Yet I sometimes astonish myself by looking at young mothers with pure envy, yearning to steady the wobbly head of a newborn, dreading menopause because it means so inarguably that I can't have any more of the babies that, God knows, *I don't want*. All of which augurs some grandmotherly atavism that might even corrupt me into baby-sitting, at least on the random weekend.

Since I haven't offered much in the way of hard-core how-to (and Professor Irwin Corey has already tied up the World's Greatest Authority title, anyway), maybe I can still pull it all together with one last assist from Chaucer. After all, when it comes to behavior in the Middle Ages, who ever knew more than he did? So here's a mock Chaucerian quatrain that I hope will synthesize this book and express my deepest feelings about life over forty.

> I telle you that ripeness is the beste.
> I vow that mydlyf's bettyr than the reste.
> I swear young folk hav naught on myddl-agyrs.
> (I swear, also, I'm Far y-Fawcett-Majyrs.)

Maybe that's still lacking something, though, by way of solid information. And perhaps I ought to explain right here that despite my reservations about advice mongers and how-to specialists in general, I didn't mean to imply that nobody has the big answers and nobody ever will. It's possible that at this very moment, some new authority is double-checking data and getting ready to unleash watchwords of guidance one can set one's life by (money back if not fully satisfied). But we'll have to keep alert. Enlightenment has a habit of beaming its laser when least expected and into the unlikeliest corners.

Take, for instance, what happened to my friend Helen at the A&P recently. Now the meat counter is the last place you'd anticipate Delphic revelation, but that's where she was, surveying the packaged wares and about to pick up some pinkish cutlets when a withered hand stayed hers. Helen traced the arresting hand to its owner, a small and quite elderly stranger who was shaking her head reprovingly. "I *happen*," said the tiny naysayer, "to be an *expert* on veal!"

Which proves, I think, that salvation may be just around the corner. After all, if there are schnitzel savants in the local supermarket, can the ultimate guide to a perfect middle age be far behind?